ENGLAND V WEST INDIES

Highlights since 1948

TEST MATCH SPECIAL TEAM

ENGLAND V WEST INDIES
Highlights since 1948

PETER BAXTER · PETER HAYTER

BBC BOOKS

✦✦✦ SPORTS EDITIONS LIMITED

Managing Director	Richard Dewing
Creative Director	Mary Hamlyn
Art Director	Rob Kelland
Senior Designer	Sandra Cowell
Design Assistant	Lyndon Brooks
Editor	Tom Whiting

First published in 1991 by BBC Books
A division of
BBC Enterprises Limited
Woodlands
80 Wood Lane
London
W12 0TT

ISBN 0-563-36232-4

Produced, edited and designed by
Sports Editions Limited
3 Greenlea Park
Prince George's Road
London
SW19 2JD

Typeset in 20th Century and Walbaum
by Sports Editions Limited
Cover origination by Clan Studios, Bromley, Kent
Black and white and colour origination by
Litho Origination Ltd, London N1
Printing and binding by BPCC Hazell Books, Aylesbury, Bucks

Contents

Acknowledgements

My thanks to Mary Hamlyn and her team of
designers at Sports Editions, particularly Rob Kelland,
and to Tom Whiting for overseeing the project.
Louise Jones and Myra Cook spent hours transcribing
hours and hours of taped transmissions, and their
efforts are greatly appreciated. I am also grateful to
Jerry Cox, Brendon Gallagher, Andrew Farrell
and Philip Stiles at Hayter's Sports Agency
for their research work on this book.
Last, but not least, thanks to Max for
being born on 28th December 1990.

PETER HAYTER · LONDON, 1991

Introduction

Broadcasting archives provide a remarkable treasure house of history, caught in the moment of its happening. Nowhere is this more true than in the recordings of live commentary or in film of events as they took place. In this book and its forerunner, which recalled celebrated moments from post-war Ashes battles, we have set ourselves the task of translating the live commentary of the time onto the printed page and supporting that with the memories of the commentators.

On these pages brief moments of glory are relived: Ramadhin and Valentine at Lord's and over a decade later David Holford on the same ground; Tom Graveney's return to the colours in 1966 and Dennis Amiss' in 1976, both at the Oval. There are even more enduring figures who stride across our scene: Gary Sobers, Colin Cowdrey, Wes Hall and Geoff Boycott, for instance.

Live, unscripted commentary, being the immediate reaction of the broadcaster to what is going on in front of him, sometimes needs a bit of 'tidying up' to make the transition into print, but we have kept that to a minimum, to recapture the moment in which it was uttered.

We are fortunate that two of our commentary team, Trevor Bailey and Fred Trueman, took part in some of the matches we are recalling and can give us the closer view from the other side of the microphone. It was just as well for us that they were on Len Hutton's memorable tour of the West Indies in 1954 and, indeed, were both successful on it, as the BBC carried no commentary on that series and so the archives are bare. Sadly, even for Test series that were fully covered, the archives have not always been kept as comprehensively stocked with commentaries as they are these days. For instance, only the end of the famous Lord's Test of 1950 remains, though older radio cricket followers may find Rex Alston's, 'Such a sight never been seen before at Lord's...' quite evocative. It has been good, too, to have Rex back on the Test Match Special team, furnishing us with his memories for this book.

Another commentary that is bound to stir memories of the circumstances in which it was heard is Alan Gibson's, 'There are two balls to go, England, needing 234 to win, are 228 for nine with Cowdrey, his left forearm in plaster, coming out to join Allen.' I know I can recall vividly sitting on the steps of a school cricket pavilion, listening to that, all thoughts of wherever I should have been completely banished. Earlier in that match came John Arlott's classic description of Ted Dexter batting against Wes Hall with 'something near majesty'.

Our selection of matches to describe is once again inevitably subjective, but certainly in one case a great match coincides with an important broadcasting milestone. Peter May and Colin Cowdrey's record stand at Edgbaston in 1957 was covered for the first time by a programme called 'Test Match Special', the name selected for that part of the old Third Network used to fill the gaps between periods of commentary on the Home Service and the Light programme. Before long, the planners had seen the advantage of disposing of the all-day ball-by-ball commentary onto that network. At the time of writing it seems likely that this long and happy association with what is now Radio Three is about to end. If so, let us hope that our relationship with our new home, Radio Five, will be as long and as happy.

In recent years, of course, West Indian domination has been almost total. I can say 'almost' because of the events of Sabina Park in Jamaica and Queen's Park Oval in Trinidad early last year. Jamaican-born Devon Malcolm's superb leg-stump yorker to dismiss Viv Richards — a crucial moment of the Kingston Test — and the cruel arrival of the rain in Port-of-Spain are both recalled here. There are times of England desperation, too. Tony Greig 'grovelling' in 1976 and in 1988 the selectors trying four captains.

Caribbean cricket has always been synonymous with flair. Even the recent years of the ruthlessly efficient four-fast-bowlers plan (now copied by any country that believes it remotely has the ammunition to do so) have not completely submerged that flair, nor, of course, the exuberant enjoyment of the game by knowledgeable West Indian supporters. The thrill we all get from witnessing great performances regardless of results puts cricket, surely, ahead of all other games.

PETER BAXTER · SOULBURY, MARCH 1991

1950 Lord's

Commentators: REX ALSTON, JOHN ARLOTT, E W SWANTON,
ROY LAWRENCE

Cricket, lovely cricket
At Lord's where I saw it.

The most famous cricket song of all is a happy Caribbean calypso, celebrating the blossoming of West Indian cricket. The seed had already been sown by the brilliant batsmanship of George Headley, Learie Constantine and the three Ws — Frank Worrell, Everton Weekes and Clyde Walcott. It was now brought to full flower, at Lord's in 1950, 'by those bowling pals of mine — Ramadhin and Valentine'.

Sonny Ramadhin and Alf Valentine, 'those two little pals of mine', bowled West Indies to their first victory over England

Ramadhin and Valentine made an extraordinary contrast. Ramadhin, a little chap in a cap with his sleeves rolled down, bowled with a lovely loose, whirlwind action. Valentine was all arms, a great character with his toothy grin. They just wheeled away all day, one of the great bowling combinations.

BRIAN JOHNSTON

Test Match Special

*T*he delightful spin bowling of Valentine and Ramadhin
provided a challenge for us commentators. Valentine
was fairly orthodox but Ramadhin was as much a mystery to
us as he was to the England batsmen.

REX ALSTON

*T*he emergence of Ramadhin and Valentine as two world-
class spinners surprised everyone. They were both just
20 and I think Ramadhin played in only five first-class
matches before the series. He bowled mainly off-breaks and
the occasional leg-cutter which was very difficult to pick. In
fact, we didn't pick him at all.

TREVOR BAILEY

Sonny Ramadhin, from Trinidad, and Alf Valentine, from Jamaica, were
on their first tour. The first Test at Old Trafford was the debut for both
of them. Even though Valentine took eight wickets in the first innings
there and eleven in the match on a dusty pitch, and Ramadhin took four
in the match, England won comfortably enough thanks to their own
spinners and were none too worried about the two youngsters who were
now about to make their first appearances at Lord's.

Trevor Bailey, Reg Simpson and Denis Compton were injured, so Len
Hutton resumed his first wicket partnership for England with Cyril
Washbrook; Alec Bedser took over Bailey's new ball duties and Gilbert
Parkhouse came into the middle order for his first Test. They were led
by Yorkshire's charming captain, Norman Yardley. At the heart of the
West Indies batting were Weekes, Worrell and Walcott.

*W*orrell, Walcott and Weekes were three batsmen in
a different class. Worrell was the most graceful,
Weekes was the best on all types of wicket, and Walcott
the most powerful. If you add Ramadhin and Valentine, it
was little wonder they did so well.

TREVOR BAILEY

The match started on Saturday 24th June, after the two sides had been
presented to King George VI. John Goddard won the toss for West Indies
and decided to bat. The openers were Allan Rae and Jeff Stollmeyer,
both later to extend their services to the game as administrators.
Stollmeyer led the way with some attacking shots, but when he had
made twenty he was lbw to Johnny Wardle's first ball — the first wicket
he had taken in a Test, in fact, with the first ball he had bowled in a
Test in England. That brought in Worrell at 37 for one and, with his
usual grace, particularly on the off-side, he quickly overhauled his more
defensive partner, Allan Rae.

Sir Frank Worrell, one of the three Ws — Worrell, Everton Weekes and Clyde Walcott

*T*he abiding memory I have of that Test was Frank Worrell getting a half volley from Bedser — and you didn't get too many of those — and late-cutting him for four. He could have hit the ball to anywhere in the ground but he chose a most exquisite shot and one that is rarely played these days.

TREVOR BAILEY

Test   Match   Special

Worrell made 52 out of a stand of 91 for the second wicket, and was eventually bowled by Bedser, but that merely brought in Weekes. He was even more aggressive in his strokeplay, taking only an hour-and-a-half to rattle up 63 before Bedser bowled him with a virtually unplayable ball — an outswinger that broke back. Approaching tea on the first day, the West Indies were already in a good position at 233 for three, and Bedser had suffered the irritation of seeing Rae dropped at slip when he had made 79. This turned into despair as Rae went on to get his hundred.

We were all delighted when Allan Rae scored a century in the first innings, he used to work with the BBC World Service so we considered him one of ours! His meticulous batting was a great contrast to the beautiful strokeplay of Worrell and the power of Walcott, who was at his very best in the second innings.

REX ALSTON

Roly Jenkins took over after tea with his leg-spinners and finally had Rae caught and bowled for 106, some revenge for the three boundaries he had taken off him in one over during the afternoon. Jenkins also induced a pair of stumpings before the close, and the next morning, after Bedser's initial breakthrough, he quickly wrapped up the tail, to finish with five for 116 from 36 overs. West Indies had not reached the sort of total that, at one stage, had seemed likely.

The West Indies opening attack consisted of the fast bowler Prior Jones and Worrell bowling medium pace. They presented little problem to Hutton and Washbrook and soon the spinners were in operation. Ramadhin and Valentine were not much less of a mystery to the West Indians than they were to England. Only the Trinidadians in the side had seen Ramadhin before the tour, and Walcott from Barbados, keeping wicket, took time to learn to read him. But Walcott was to claim the first wicket — Hutton, stumped off Valentine for 35. It was an unusual way for Hutton to get out, and many years later he admitted that he had fancied his chances against Valentine.

But now it was Ramadhin who started making inroads, having Washbrook stumped for 36, Edrich caught behind for 8 and Doggart lbw for a duck.

Ramadhin basically bowled a ball that came in a little bit and everybody played for the off-break, but now and again he produced the leg-break which no-one could see. We discovered up at Nottingham that sometimes, when he turned round, he stroked the back of his cap, and when he did, that the ball usually went from leg to off. When

Test Match Special

13

interviewing Goddard, we put it to him that this was a signal to the wicketkeeper Walcott, and he said, 'Oh no, of course it isn't.' But we told the England batsmen, and from then on they played him rather well.

BRIAN JOHNSTON

But today Ramadhin was a real problem. Norman Yardley's view later was that the damage was done in the dressing room as waiting batsmen pondered how to play the little wizard. Yardley himself was bowled by Valentine for 16 and Parkhouse went the same way for a duck in his first Test innings. Ramadhin bowled both Evans and Bedser and Valentine had Jenkins caught behind. Nine wickets had gone down for the addition of only sixty runs. Bob Berry hung on while Wardle laid about the attack, hitting six boundaries in 33 runs, before Jones was brought back to account for Berry. England were all out for what was then their lowest score against West Indies — a paltry 151. Ramadhin and Valentine had done the majority of the bowling — 88 overs between them. By the end, Ramadhin had taken five for 66 and Valentine four for 48.

West Indies started their second innings with a lead of 175, but the perseverance of Jenkins again maintained a measure of control. Rae, Stollmeyer, Worrell and Goddard all fell to him and, at 146 for four, West Indies were not out of sight.

I wonder how many modern day cricket followers have heard or read about Worcestershire's Roly Jenkins — he had match figures of nine for 290 off 94.2 overs and was comfortably England's best bowler. He was a great comedian and with Johnny Wardle also in the team I suspect England will have enjoyed a few laughs despite their defeat.

REX ALSTON

Weekes was run out for 63 after a mid-pitch mix-up with Walcott with whom he had added 53 for the fifth wicket. Crucially, Walcott had already been missed at slip off Edrich, a mistake for which he was going to make England pay. He was now joined by the all-rounder Gerry Gomez who gave him great support, but it was Walcott's day.

It was the first time that I had seen him and the great power of his defensive strokes. I would never have dreamt of fielding at silly mid-on or silly mid-off to him. He was very powerful off the back foot, one of the most powerful batsmen I have ever seen.

BRIAN JOHNSTON

Commentators have always talked about Walcott's strength, and rightly so, but his classical straight driving was my abiding memory of his 168 not out.

REX ALSTON

With Gomez making 70, Walcott added 211 for the sixth wicket. Their stand broke England, and not long after Bedser had finally claimed Gomez's wicket, the lead reached 600 and Goddard declared. England had been left the best part of two days to score 601 to win. Ramadhin and Valentine were soon in action again and, when the score had reached only 26, Hutton left what turned out to be Valentine's arm ball and was bowled for 10. Edrich became Ramadhin's first victim of this innings as the bowler used the dark background of the pavilion — no sightscreen at that end in those days — as an aid to bamboozle the batsmen. But he had to work for his wickets on that fourth day. Doggart shared a third wicket stand of 83 with Washbrook before Ramadhin bowled him for 25 and Parkhouse atoned for his first innings duck with 48 out of a fourth wicket stand of 78 during which Washbrook reached his hundred. But just before the close, Valentine had Parkhouse caught at silly mid-off. It was 218 for four, a disappointing end to the day, but England still had six wickets standing with which to try to survive the final day. Moreover, Washbrook was 114 not out.

Unfortunately, Washbrook went next morning, yorked by Ramadhin, before he had added to that score and the writing was on the wall. Valentine took the wicket of Yardley for the second time in the match, and then Ramadhin ran through Evans, Jenkins and Bedser before

Cyril Washbrook hits to leg during his second innings hundred. Wicket-keeper Clyde Walcott, whose unbeaten 168 set up West Indies winning total of 425, looks on

Test Match Special

After the heroics of Ramadhin and Valentine had made victory certain, Worrell struck to trap Johnny Wardle leg-before and end the match

Wardle, as he had in the first innings, decided to lay about him for some last-ditch resistance.

REX ALSTON *Well now Valentine has been knocked off by Wardle and Worrell is taking his place. Worrell is going to bowl from this Pavilion end. Worrell comes up, he bowls to Wardle. Wardle's quite content to play that straight back down the wicket and he's still got Williams on the deep square-leg boundary, three men fairly close in on the leg side one at mid-on and two close in near the wicket. Wardle, forward defensive stroke. Wardle not out 21 pushes that one to Goddard who's at extra cover, short extra cover. He's not silly mid-off any longer, he's gone back, he's the best part of 20 yards from the bat. Worrell bowls and an almighty sweep and he's out lbw...Wardle is lbw, snatches the stump and the players are running off the field, and here come the ground staff to prevent an encroachment of the wicket. There are one or two West Indian characters coming out on the field waving their hats as the West Indies players walk quietly off the field. Yes, there are several West Indian supporters running from the far end and they are going to escort their team off the field. The score is 274. Goddard running in with his stump being chased harem scarem by lots of West Indian supporters. Such a sight never been seen before at Lord's.*

There were great celebrations when they gained their first victory in England at Lord's. It established them outside their own country and Ramadhin and Valentine became celebrities.

T R E V O R   B A I L E Y

The outstanding memory, of course, was the calypso at the end led by Lord Kitchener doing some sort of dance. It was certainly the first time one had seen an invasion of Lord's except in Eton and Harrow matches where everyone used to crowd on the field. But for them to come and sing calypsos in front of the old members' pavilion was really quite something. It really was, it was sensational.

B R I A N   J O H N S T O N

REX ALSTON *They are determined, I think, to give us a little song...a band of about a dozen of them. One in a bright red cap, one in a bright blue shirt and they are dancing out into the middle and there is a press photographer chasing after them but I think they will be herded tactfully off the middle. In fact, there is a policeman now telling them to go away and they are singing and dancing off the pitch and the English section of the spectators is giving them a round of applause.*

The West Indies had won by 326 runs and the little West Indian pair now had such a hold on England's batting that the remaining two Tests went their way as well — at Trent Bridge by ten wickets and at the Oval by an innings and 56 runs.

Valentine finished the four-Test series with 33 wickets and Ramadhin with 25. Here at Lord's, Ramadhin had taken eleven wickets and Valentine seven. As the song goes:

The bowling was superfine — Ramadhin and Valentine.

Strangely, the only game we won was on a real turner in the first Test. It was a beach at Old Trafford and our victory there made our failure in the second Test all the more surprising to us.

Our failure to play Ramadhin and Valentine was our downfall. We never really got it right during that series. The West Indies used only 12 men in the Tests but we used 25, and many were not good enough.

T R E V O R   B A I L E Y

Test   Match   Special

FINAL · SCORES

WEST INDIES - First Innings

A F Rae, c and b Jenkins		106
J B Stollmeyer, lbw b Wardle		20
F M Worrell, b Bedser		52
E Weekes, b Bedser		63
C L Walcott, st Evans b Jenkins		14
G E Gomez, st Evans b Jenkins		1
R J Christiani, b Bedser		33
J D Goddard, b Wardle		14
P E Jones, c Evans b Jenkins		0
S Ramadhin, not out		1
A L Valentine, c Hutton b Jenkins		5
Extras (b10, lb5, w1, nb1)		17
Total		**326**

Fall of wickets: 1-37, 2-128, 3-233, 4-262, 5-273, 6-274, 7-320, 8-320, 9-320
Bowling: Bedser 40-14-60-3, Edrich 16-4-30-0, Jenkins 35.2-6-116-5, Wardle 17-6-46-2, Berry 19-7-45-0, Yardley 4-1-12-0

ENGLAND - First Innings

L Hutton, st Walcott b Valentine		35
C Washbrook, st Walcott b Ramadhin		36
W J Edrich, c Walcott b Ramadhin		8
G H G Doggart, lbw b Ramadhin		0
W G A Parkhouse, b Valentine		0
N W D Yardley, b Valentine		16
T G Evans, b Ramadhin		8
R O Jenkins, c Walcott b Valentine		4
J H Wardle, not out		33
A V Bedser, b Ramadhin		5
R Berry, c Goddard b Jones		2
Extras (b2, lb1, w1)		4
Total		**151**

Fall of wickets: 1-62, 2-74, 3-74, 4-75, 5-86, 6-102, 7-110, 8-113, 9-122
Bowling: Jones 8.4-2-13-1, Worrell 10-4-20-0, Valentine 45-28-48-4, Ramadhin 43-27-66-5

WEST INDIES - Second Innings

A F Rae, b Jenkins		24
J B Stollmeyer, b Jenkins		30
F M Worrell, c Doggard b Jenkins		45
E Weekes, run out		63
C L Walcott, not out		168
G E Gomez, c Edrich b Bedser		70
R J Christiani, not out		5
J D Goddard, c Evans b Jenkins		11
Extras (lb8, nb1)		9
Total (6 wkts dec)		**425**

Fall of wickets: 1-48, 2-75, 3-108, 4-146, 5-199, 6-410
Bowling: Bedser 44-16-80-1, Edrich 13-2-37-0, Jenkins 59-13-174-4, Wardle 30-10-58-0, Berry 32-15-67-0

ENGLAND - Second Innings

L Hutton, b Valentine		10
C Washbrook, b Ramadhin		114
W J Edrich, c Jones b Ramadhin		8
G H G Doggart, b Ramadhin		25
W G A Parkhouse, c Goddard b Valentine		48
N W D Yardley, c Weekes b Valentine		19
T G Evans, c Rae b Ramadhin		2
R O Jenkins, b Ramadhin		4
J H Wardle, lbw b Worrell		21
A V Bedser, b Ramadhin		0
R Berry, not out		0
Extras (b2, lb1, w1)		23
Total		**274**

Fall of wickets: 1-28, 2-57, 3-140, 4-218, 5-228, 6-238, 7-245, 8-258, 9-258
Bowling: Jones 7-1-22-0, Worrell 23.3-9-39-1, Valentine 71-47-79-3, Ramadhin 72-43-86-6, Gomez 13-1-25-0, Goddard 6-6-0-0

West Indies won by 326 runs.

West Indies supporters invade the Lord's pitch to celebrate their team's first victory over England, calypso-style

Test Match Special

1954 Sabina Park

FIFTH TEST, 30, 31 MARCH, 1-3 APRIL

There were two Test matches at Sabina Park in 1954. In the first — the first Test of the series — Ramadhin and Valentine again cast their spell, taking seven first innings wickets between them. England, led by Len Hutton, eventually fell 140 runs short of a target of 457. Their defeat in the Second Test in Barbados was by a larger margin, thanks to a double century in the first innings from Clyde Walcott and the little pals hauling in another seven wickets between them to ensure England faced a first innings deficit of 202. An innings of 166 from John Holt gave Jeff Stollmeyer the chance to declare again, this time setting England 495 to win. They were bowled out 181 runs short. It was getting to be a repetitive business.

The MCC party went on to British Guiana (now Guyana) knowing that they really had to win to stay in the series. There was some trouble finding an umpire for the match. Unpopular decisions — as when Holt had been given out lbw in Jamaica, his own island, six runs short of a maiden Test century — had tended to make an umpire's life no sinecure. To Hutton's surprise, the local club president ordered his groundsman, a man named Menzies, to stand in that third Test. He was to have a major incident to deal with, but the most important change for the touring team in Georgetown was that Hutton won the toss and he himself made 169 of a total of 435. Now the positions were reversed. Brian Statham took four West Indies wickets, but an eighth wicket stand between Holt and Clifford McWatt put on 99 before it was ended by a run out. The wretched umpire called on for an apparently straightforward decision was Menzies, who found himself at the centre of something of a riot. However, Hutton prevailed on him to stay on the field and the West Indies were soon following on, 184 runs behind.

All the bowlers had a hand in dismissing them a second time in the 250s and, after knocking off the 72 runs that were needed to win for the loss of only one wicket, England found themselves now only 2-1 down.

In Trinidad, though, the three Ws got to work. Weekes 206, Worrell 167 and Walcott 124 in a total of 681 for eight. Centuries from May and Compton ensured that there was no capitulation and, despite a first innings deficit of 144, England saved the game comfortably enough. So they returned north west to Jamaica.

We had to win at Sabina Park. We were 2-1 down in the series and so we had to ask: 'What can we do?' Brian Statham, our best bowler, was injured and the pitch

It's bon voyage as the England tour party depart for the Caribbean under the leadership of Len Hutton (bottom left). The visitors started badly but fought back well to draw the series 2-2, with Hutton himself topping the batting averages with 96.71

was flat and glistening — an absolute beauty. So we all sat down and tried to devise a strategy. Eventually we decided that our best plan was to win the toss, make a lot of runs, and hope later that Lock and Wardle would bowl them out.

But Len Hutton lost the toss and we were all very depressed when he came back to the dressing room. Our thoughts were: 'We're bound to lose. With the strength of their batting and with such a fine pitch, there is no way we can win.'

Test Match Special

Fred Trueman bowling to Jeff Stollmeyer on the first morning of the fifth Test at a sunny Sabina Park

We took the field and I was to open the bowling in place of Statham. Because I can't generate away swing, I like to bowl with a cross wind. But Fred Trueman wanted to bowl with the wind behind him, so we planned to alternate during our spells.

So I began bowling into the wind and suddenly wickets started falling. Now, I would have settled for three for 100 at the start of the day. There was no reason why anything untoward should happen but I was moving the ball a little bit all the time.

TREVOR BAILEY

Trevor Bailey bowled absolutely beautifully, using the seam and the moisture in the ground.

FRED TRUEMAN

Test Match Special

With his fifth ball, Bailey had the dangerous Holt caught at short leg and with only two on the board he captured the most dangerous batsman of all, Everton Weekes, bowled by what Trevor delights in describing as 'the nip-backer'. He then had Stollmeyer caught behind for 9 and Trueman followed that with two short balls to Worrell, off the second of which he was caught at short leg. Incredibly, the West Indies were 13 for four and Bailey had taken three for 5. There was, of course, a third 'W' and Walcott added 52 with Denis Atkinson to halt the rot to some extent. Lock then removed Walcott, but there were four more wickets for Bailey, who recorded his best Test figures.

They collapsed for 139, which was totally unexpected. It was my best Test performance as a bowler and it was all the more surprising because I was bowling at the end I didn't want to bowl from.

But instead of it being all over for the day, I went in to bat for the last 35 minutes. I accompanied Len Hutton as an emergency opener and we saw the day out. Len went on to make a double hundred and he didn't give a chance — an absolutely superb innings.

I made 23 before I was caught off Sobers, which made me his first Test victim. It was Sobers' first Test. He was replacing Valentine, who was injured. He went in at number nine — that's quite a number nine to have in your side. He was going in at number six for Barbados, and if you do that you can really bat. He was only bowling slow left arm but you could tell he was going to be something special.

TREVOR BAILEY

So Trevor Bailey became the first of Sobers' 235 Test wickets (and eventually also his biographer). But, crucially, Hutton and Bailey had batted through to lunch on the second day and the pitch was now becoming easier. May joined Hutton and they took the score past 100 before Ramadhin had Peter May caught for 30. Batting was not easy, especially in the face of some hostile fast bowling from Frank King who had Compton out hit wicket for 30 as he tried to avoid a bumper. Willie Watson went soon after, caught behind off King and with Atkinson having Graveney lbw, England were quite glad to see the close of play with five wickets down and the lead past 50. The great thing was that Hutton had batted through the day and was still there. The 21 furious overs that King had bowled on that second day had exacted a price. The next day he was out of the attack with a strained muscle in his leg. Hutton, though, carried on past his hundred and received valuable support from Evans

Trevor Bailey gave an immaculate exhibition of controlled swing bowling

who made 28 of a stand of 108, and from Wardle, with 66 of a seventh wicket stand of 105, which took England to the verge of 400 and Hutton to the first double hundred by an England captain overseas.

It was a magnificent innings. I remember he hit Gary Sobers clean out of the ground for a straight six over where the George Headley Stand is now. It was a magnificent shot and I can remember the bowler standing there shading his eyes as the ball went away into the the distance. He was completely drained through concentration, which led to one little incident. When he came off the field the Jamaican Prime Minister, Sir Alexander Bustamante, was there. Leonard didn't recognise him in his shirtsleeves and pushed by him — not with intent, he just wanted to get into the cool of the dressing room. The local newspaper men made a bit of a thing of that, but Leonard did apologise when he found out who he was.

FRED TRUEMAN

With a lead of 275, Trueman showed that he, too, could be fast, furious and accurate. He took three of the first four wickets, including Stollmeyer for 64, and the West Indies were 123 for four and in danger of losing by an innings, especially with two of the three Ws out. But Walcott resisted strongly, adding 68 for the fifth wicket with Gomez who made 22 of them and then 82 for the sixth wicket with Atkinson who made 40. With his score in the nineties, though, Walcott received a blow on the wrist which hampered him severely, yet he managed to take West Indies into the lead and himself to a fine hundred before Jim Laker claimed him as one of four wickets from a 50 over spell of teasing off-spin. England needed only 72 to win on a pitch which had just been freshened by a short shower. That may have contributed to the loss of Graveney in the first over as he opened with Watson, but although there were a few more alarms, May and Watson saw England home to a remarkable nine-wicket win inside five days of the six-day Test.

No-one was more surprised at winning than we were, especially after our original strategy had been completely wrecked.

TREVOR BAILEY

FINAL · SCORES

WEST INDIES - First Innings

J K Holt, c Lock b Bailey	0
J B Stollmeyer, c Evans b Bailey	9
E de C Weekes, b Bailey	0
F M M Worrell, c Wardle b Trueman	4
C L Walcott, c Laker b Lock	50
D St E Atkinson, lbw b Bailey	21
G E Gomez, c Watson b Bailey	4
C A McWatt, c Lock b Bailey	22
G St A Sobers, not out	14
F M King, b Bailey	9
S Ramadhin, lbw b Trueman	4
Extras (lb1 nb1)	2
Total	**139**

Fall of wickets: 1-0, 2-2, 3-13, 4-13, 5-65, 6-75, 7-110, 8-115, 9-133
Bowling: Bailey 16-7-34-7, Trueman 15.4-4-39-2, Wardle 10-1-20-0, Lock 15-6-31-1, Laker 4-1-13-0

ENGLAND - First Innings

L Hutton, c McWatt b Walcott	205
T E Bailey, c McWatt b Sobers	23
P B H May, c sub (B H Pairaudeau) b Ramadhin	30
D C S Compton, hit wkt b King	31
W Watson, c McWatt b King	4
T W Graveney, lbw b Atkinson	11
T G Evans, c Worrell b Ramadhin	28
J H Wardle, c Hold b Sobers	66
G A R Lock, b Sobers	4
J C Laker, b Sobers	9
F S Trueman, not out	0
Extras (lb3)	3
Total	**414**

Fall of wickets: 1-43, 2-104, 3-152, 4-160, 5-179, 6-287, 7-392, 8-401, 9-406
Bowling: King 26-12-45-2, Gomez 25-8-56-0, Atkinson 41-15-82-1, Ramadhin 29-9-71-2, Sobers 28.5-9-75-4, Walcott 11-5-26-1, Worrell 11-0-34-0, Stollmeyer 5-0-22-0

WEST INDIES - Second Innings

J K Holt, c Lock b Trueman	8
J B Stollmeyer, lbw b Trueman	6
E de C Weekes, b Wardle	3
F M M Worrell, c Graveney b Trueman	29
C L Walcott, c Graveney b Laker	116
G E Gomez, lbw b Laker	22
D St E Atkinson, c Watson b Bailey	40
C A McWatt, c Wardle b Laker	8
G St A Sobers, c Compton b Lock	26
S Ramadhin, c and b Laker	10
F M King, not out	10
Extras (b4, lb3, w1, nb2)	10
Total	**346**

Fall of wickets: 1-26, 2-38, 3-102, 4-123, 5-191, 6-273, 7-293, 8-306, 9-326
Bowling: Bailey 25-11-54-1, Trueman 29-7-88-3, Wardle 39-14-83-1, Lock 27-16-40-1, Laker 50-27-71-4

ENGLAND - Second Innings

T W Graveney, b King	0
P B H May, not out	40
W Watson, not out	20
Extras (b12)	12
Total (1 wkt)	**72**

Fall of wickets: 1-0
Bowling: King 4-1-21-1, Atkinson 3-0-8-0, Ramadhin 3-0-14-0, Sobers 1-0-6-0, Worrell 4-0-8-0, Weekes 0.5-0-3-0

England won by 9 wickets

A 50-over spell of teasing off-spin allowed Jim Laker to claim four invaluable wickets in West Indies second innings

1957 Edgbaston

FIRST TEST, 30, 31 MAY, 1, 3, 4 JUNE

Commentators: REX ALSTON, JOHN ARLOTT, E W SWANTON
AND KEN ABLACK
Summarisers: GERRY GOMEZ

This was an historic occasion for the BBC. It was the first Test broadcast ball-by-ball in England through the introduction of the Third Network to fill the gaps in coverage on the Home Service and Light Programme, the forerunners of Radios 4 and 2. The new service, publicised with the slogan 'Don't miss a ball, we broadcast them all' bore, for the first time, the title *Test Match Special.*

The terrible trio of Swanton, Arlott and Alston were housed in a splendid new box. Myself and Swanton were stricken with sore throats and I fear we rather overdid our pleas for sympathy. Throat lozenges and herbal potions arrived by the sackful from concerned listeners, perhaps setting a precedent for Brian Johnston's infamous cakes. I can't understand why we were ill. Two wonderful blind ladies, Dora and Eileen Turner, used to knit the commentary team wonderful warm woollen socks and scarves to ward off the English 'summer'. There was no conceivable excuse for catching a cold.

REX ALSTON

It was to be an historic test, too, for cricketing reasons, with a fairly substantial bogey of a bowler laid. There had not been a Test at Edgbaston for 28 years. Now it was selected for the first Test of a new series and the return of the West Indies, the three Ws, Ramadhin, Valentine and all. England were captained by Peter May, who had one of the best balanced attacks England can ever have fielded: Fred Trueman, Brian Statham, Trevor Bailey, Jim Laker and Tony Lock.

On paper they were just as talented a side as the one that toured previously in 1950. But I think we were a much better side, probably the best in the world. May had become a world-class player, Cowdrey was outstanding and Statham was a superb bowler.
We had also learned to play Ramadhin rather better.

TREVOR BAILEY

Test   Match   Special

The match started unusually early this year, on the 30th May in fine weather conditions on a good pitch. May had no hesitation in batting when he won the toss. He and his batsmen had decided that the way they would play Ramadhin would be to attack him, but the first problem they had to contend with was a new young fast bowler in his first Test, the fiery Roy Gilchrist. It was he who removed Brian Close, opening with Peter Richardson, caught behind by another new cap, Rohan Kanhai, for 15.

Doug Insole joined Richardson, who was beginning to think in terms of a Test fifty when Ramadhin was introduced and had him caught close to the wicket for 47. There was still no hint of the carnage to come as Insole and May took the score past 100. But Ramadhin had found a little moisture in the pitch which was helping him to turn the ball and skid

The Steel Band Skiffle Group were in lively musical form at Edgbaston prior to the start of the first day's play

T e s t   M a t c h   S p e c i a l

Sonny Ramadhin's ability to disguise his leg-cutter caused consternation for England's batsmen

some onto the batsman. Now he had more success, bowling Insole for 20 and having May caught at slip for 30. At 115 for four, England had two new batsmen in with Bailey now joining Cowdrey.

I played him on a turner the first time I'd seen him. It turned square and I got a sort of feeling. I could never exactly pick him, but thought I knew basically which way the ball was going to go. The West Indies themselves couldn't understand why we couldn't pick his leg-cutter from his normal off-break. I always found it difficult, but in the end I tried to scent it, rather than pick it. I played him all the time as an off-spinner but I reckoned that when he threw the ball high in the air that was probably the leg-cutter. The reason was that he never bowled a quick leg-cutter because it wouldn't have turned.

TREVOR BAILEY

KEN ABLACK *The field being set for Bailey, Ramadhin's having a word with Goddard. The offside field is now one slip, a man at point square with the wicket, cover and mid-off. Ramadhin, bowling over the wicket to Bailey, runs in and bowls, pitches it right up and Bailey just moves forward and plays it dead down in front of him and Goddard has to take two steps forward from silly mid-on to pick the ball up. 116 for four. Ramadhin to Bailey, shorter and that one off the inside edge. Sobers throws himself across to the left, gets a hand to it, Ramadhin holds his head. Gerry Gomez, was that a catch?*

GERRY GOMEZ *No, it dropped short of him Ken, off the inside edge — a quicker one.*

KEN ABLACK *Now Ramadhin again to Bailey, Bailey forward and he's bowled!*

GERRY GOMEZ *It was an off-spinner flighted much slower than the previous ball, which had hurried through, and Bailey. . . frankly, having played against Bailey quite a few times, I've never seen him more conclusively bowled than on this occasion. I think that Bailey will admit that its one of the better balls that he has received in his Test cricket career. He was beaten in the flight where he started moving forward to the pitch of it but never got there and it hit the off stump. It was a beautiful piece of bowling by Ramadhin, a beautiful variation of pace from the previous ball and this innings so far is all Ramadhin on a wicket which I don't think is yet his piece of cake really.*

KEN ABLACK *Well, what a sudden dramatic change England 93 for two at lunch, now 116 for five. Ramadhin right on top.*

Test Match Special

The next man in was Lock, who was bowled by Ramadhin for nought. Cowdrey decided on attack and was caught in the deep for 4 and Laker was Ramadhin's seventh victim, bowled for 7. England had slumped from 104 for two to 130 for eight. There was a minor revival from the last two wickets which added 56, including Trueman's 29 not out. England had been bowled out in four hours for 186 and Ramadhin, this time without Valentine, who had been left out, had taken seven for 49 in 31 overs and had weaved his old magic again.

The West Indies started their reply after tea on the first day and lost Pairaudeau yorked by Trueman in his second over. But that was the limit of England's success that day and, at the close, West Indies were only 103 behind at 83 for one. Without a run added on the Friday morning, Statham had Kanhai lbw for 42 and Weekes came in to join Walcott, a sight to shake the spirits of most bowlers. However, Walcott was soon in trouble, though not at the bowler's hands. He pulled a muscle going for a quick single and had to continue batting with a runner. But even thus handicapped he continued to show his tremendous power, picking the right ball to hit. He lost Weekes, bowled by Trueman for nine, but he hit 11 boundaries on his way to 90, on which score he was caught behind off Laker. His partner during the fourth wicket stand of 63 which had taken the West Indies very nearly into the lead, was the young Gary Sobers. He was now joined by his great friend, 'Collie' Smith. Sobers himself was soon out to a hard cut at Statham, which produced a fine diving catch by Bailey at slip. Sobers was gone for 53, but Worrell came in to face the second new ball against the England bowling attack of Trueman and Statham.

On his debut against England, Collie Smith hit an impressive 161

It was twenty past three on the second afternoon. The lead was still slender with half the side out and these two great bowlers were beating the bat regularly. It was Smith's first Test appearance against England, but his confidence increased with the elegant Worrell at the other end. The lead grew and their sixth wicket stand stretched into Saturday as Smith reached his century in front of a crowd of 32,000. 'Collie' Smith would probably have become one of the great names of West Indian cricket, but he was to die tragically two years later in a car crash while playing league cricket in England.

As lunch approached on that third day, Worrell had to call for a runner. He was eventually bowled by Statham right at the end of the morning session for 81 of a sixth-wicket stand of 190. It was 387 for six and the West Indies were in command. John Goddard, the captain, helped Smith add 79 for the seventh wicket, falling to Laker for 24 and soon after that Laker ended Smith's magnificent innings, lbw for 161. The tail contributed little and the West Indies were all out in the middle of the third afternoon for 474, a lead of 288. After their first innings

Peter Richardson, the England opener, is caught by substitute Nyron Asgarali off Ramadhin for 34

collapse, England were not optimistic.

Richardson and Close weathered the opening storm from Gilchrist, reducing the deficit by 63 runs. Again, though, it was Ramadhin who set England back on their heels. In successive overs he removed Richardson for 34 and Insole for nought. It was 65 for two as May came in to join Close, determined not to look at the scoreboard which would have showed him that his side was still over 200 runs behind. Almost immediately he drove Ramadhin through the covers to boost his own morale, even though he had to admit to himself that he had no idea whether the ball had been the leg- or the off-break.

May and Close saw out the rest of Saturday's play and had added 48 when, on Monday morning, Gilchrist had Close caught at slip for 42. The best part of two days lay ahead and they were still 175 runs behind as Colin Cowdrey joined May and one of the most remarkable partnerships in cricket history was forged. Ramadhin wheeled away at the two Englishmen, mystifying them regularly. He bowled 48 overs that day with no more than moral success, and at a cost of less than two an over. With the lbw law as it was then, May and Cowdrey in particular were able to pad the ball away with impunity if it pitched outside the off stump. Sonny Ramadhin reckoned that he appealed over a hundred times that day, to no avail.

*F*or me, preparing to go in, the effect of so many shouts was unnerving. I kept getting out of my seat every time an appeal went up, thinking I was about to go in. There were so many calls because then you could pad up to balls on the off stump. Cowdrey, in particular, would stick his left leg right down the pitch and pad the ball away.

Ramadhin had bowled very well in the first innings, getting seven for 49. But he was bowled too much in the second innings. He bowled 98 overs with little success. It was a definite error of captaincy to keep him on so long. It emasculated him.

TREVOR BAILEY

*T*he marathon Cowdrey-May partnership was not easy to commentate on. There are only so many ways of describing exactly the same shot or delivery. Keeping the dialogue fresh was a great challenge.

REX ALSTON

May, scoring more quickly, reached his hundred after four hours and ten minutes . . . and on they went. At the close of the fourth day they had made sure that the West Indies would have to bat again. They were 378 for three, having added 265, for a lead now of 90. May was 193 and Cowdrey 78.

Already without the medium pace of Worrell, the West Indies now also lost Gilchrist to injury. So, as the match went into the final day, there was a lot of bowling for Ramadhin and Atkinson — with his off-cutters and off-breaks — to get through. For the first and only time in his career, that morning Peter May reached a double century. Cowdrey, admiring his friend and captain from the other end, had no doubt that it was the greatest innings he had ever witnessed. He, too, reached his hundred and on they went, Cowdrey now opening up to play with greater freedom.

REX ALSTON *And England must be looking for runs now. Smith bowls short, Cowdrey has placed it gently towards third man, and the extra applause is because the partnership is now worth a monumental figure of 400. I think the imagination starts to boggle at all this business about records. We're getting tired of it, I should think Roy Webber is drooling records, somewhere else along in this box. There must have been higher records. What is the highest partnership? Now, Jack Price here's a problem for you: What's the highest partnership by a couple of Englishmen in a Test match in England? You can work that one out quietly, while Sobers starts the fresh over with the score 513 for three. And Sobers bowls to Cowdrey, and he draws away and forces it off the back foot, and*

T e s t   M a t c h   S p e c i a l

Ramadhin fields very deep at third man. One run to Cowdrey, he's now scored 153, and now May, 247, faces Sobers and May has hit the next one high in the air. . .it's six, into the Pavilion, just over mid-on and he's also scored a mere 250, 253 to be precise. Sobers bowls to him again and May has waited for that, which was a half volley, very well pitched up and very wide of the off-stump and May flashes the bat and it goes to Ramadhin at third man. May 254, England 521 for three.

With his score on 154, Cowdrey at last hit one in the air to the substitute fielder, Nyron Asgarali, off the bowling of Smith and the marathon stand was over. They had added 411, which to this day

Colin Cowdrey (left) hit 154 and Peter May 285 not out in their record 4th wicket stand of 411

remains England's highest partnership for any wicket and the world record for the fourth wicket. Meanwhile, Trevor Bailey had set up his own record. . .

I had my pads on in the first Test at Edgbaston for the longest time probably any cricketer has ever worn them. I sat for two days in the dressing room watching with my pads on. I like to sit and watch the game when I'm next in, but not for two days! In fact, I never went in, I think I was dead by that time. That's what I remember most about the game — sitting in the dressing room.

TREVOR BAILEY

So, at 524 for four, with a lead of 236, in came the ebullient England wicket-keeper, Godfrey Evans.

We all got excited towards the end of the England second innings when we felt an earlier declaration could have increased the chances of an England victory. I am convinced that Peter May, still batting away in the middle, was too exhausted to make a clear-cut decision.

REX ALSTON

May and Evans batted together for another half hour, boosting the total by another 59 runs before May declared, the exhausted batsman having to ask the umpires how far ahead they were. The answer was, at 583 for four, a total of 295 runs. May himself had batted for little short of 10 hours for the highest score of his first-class career, 285 not out.

The fact that the declaration may have been a bit too late was now shown up as the tired West Indians quickly found themselves in trouble. Trueman had both openers back in the pavilion with only nine runs on the board, and then Laker and Lock found the ball turning for them. Lock picked up the wickets of Sobers, Worrell and Weekes and Laker sent back Walcott and Smith. Suddenly England were pressing for what would have been a remarkable win with the West Indies at 68 for seven. In the end, there was not enough time and the match was drawn.

Having looked certain winners at Edgbaston, the West Indies were to go on to lose the series 3-0.

They never really recovered from that. They drew instead of winning and could so easily have lost. The West Indies were torn by internal strife. The rivalry between islands was stronger than it is now, and there was also great hostility between black and white in the side.

TREVOR BAILEY

Test Match Special

FINAL · SCORES

ENGLAND - First Innings

P E Richardson, c Walcott b Ramadhin	47
D B Close, c Rohan Kanhai b Gilchrist	15
D J Insole, b Ramadhin	20
P B H May, c Weekes b Ramadhin	30
M C Cowdrey, c Gilchrist b Ramadhin	4
T E Bailey, b Ramadhin	1
G A R Lock, b Ramadhin	0
T G Evans, b Gilchrist	14
J C Laker, b Ramadhin	7
F S Trueman, not out	29
J B Statham, b Atkinson	13
Extras (b3, lb3)	6
Total	186

Fall of wickets: 1-32, 2-61, 3-104, 4-115, 5-116, 6-118, 7-121, 8-130, 9-150
Bowling: Worrell 9-1-27-0, Gilchrist 27-4-74-2, Ramadhin 31-16-49-7, Atkinson 12.4-3-30-1

WEST INDIES - First Innings

Rohan Kanhai, lbw b Statham	42
B H Pairaudeau, b Trueman	1
C L Walcott, c Evans b Laker	90
E D Weekes, b Trueman	9
G Sobers, c Bailey b Statham	53
O G Smith, lbw b Laker	161
F M Worrell, b Statham	81
J D Goddard, c Lock b Laker	24
D Atkinson, c Statham b Laker	1
S Ramadhin, not out	5
R Gilchrist, run out	0
Extras (b1, lb6)	7
Total	474

Fall of wickets: 1-4, 2-83, 3-120, 4-183, 5-197, 6-387, 7-466, 8-469, 9-474
Bowling: Statham 39-4-114-3, Trueman 30-4-99-2, Bailey 34-11-80-0, Laker 54-17-119-4, Lock 34.4-15-55-0

ENGLAND - Second Innings

P E Richardson, c sub b Ramadhin	34
D B Close, c Weekes b Gilchrist	42
D J Insole, b Ramadhin	0
P B H May, not out	285
M C Cowdrey, c sub b Smith	154
T G Evans, not out	29
Extras (b23, lb16)	39
Total (4 wkts dec)	583

Fall of wickets: 1-63, 2-65, 3-113, 4-524
Bowling: Gilchrist 26-2-67-1, Ramadhin 98-35-179-2, Atkinson 72-29-137-0, Sobers 30-4-77-0, Smith 26-4-72-1, Goddard 6-2-12-0

WEST INDIES - Second Innings

Rohan Kanhai, c Close b Trueman	7
B H Pairaudeau, b Trueman	1
C L Walcott, c Lock b Laker	7
E D Weekes, c Trueman b Lock	33
G Sobers, c Cowdrey b Lock	14
O G Smith, lbw b Laker	5
F M Worrell, c May b Lock	0
J D Goddard, not out	0
D Atkinson, not out	4
Extras (b7)	7
Total (7 wkts)	72

Fall of wickets: 1-1, 2-9, 3-25, 4-27, 5-43, 6-66, 7-68
Bowling: Statham 2-0-6-0, Trueman 5-3-7-2, Laker 24-20-13-2, Lock 2-1-8-0, Close 2-1-8-0

Match drawn

Peter May bids farewell to the 1957 West Indies at Waterloo Station as they begin their journey home

Test Match Special

1960 Queen's Park Oval

SECOND TEST, 28-30 JANUARY, 1-3 FEBRUARY

The banana boat that made a rough crossing of the Atlantic to the Caribbean in late December 1959 carried in it a confident England side under the leadership of Peter May. They had just completed a 5-0 whitewash of India at home and, though they knew the West Indies were liable to be a tougher nut to crack, in May himself, Colin Cowdrey, Ted Dexter and Ken Barrington, they had some strong batting while Trueman and Statham were in their pomp; and they had Ray Illingworth and David Allen to spin the ball. The First Test was in Barbados, where England had just lost to the island side for whom Seymour Nurse hit a double century.

In the Test, it was Sobers who made a double century, while Frank Worrell — in his own island — was 197 when Gerry Alexander declared. A brave man. The West Indies by that time had made 563 for eight, replying to England's 482 in which Dexter and Barrington made hundreds, but the match was drawn. And so south to Trinidad.

The Queen's Park Oval pitch was faster than the one in Bridgetown had been, and England were relieved to have Statham back from an injury that had caused him to miss the First Test. However, the West Indies themselves had an extremely fast combination to take the new ball in Wes Hall and Chester Watson. Facing them, after May had won the toss, was the new opening pair for England of Geoff Pullar and Colin Cowdrey. After half an hour, Hall and Watson changed ends and subjected the batsmen to an all-out assault of short-pitched bowling that produced the breakthrough. Watson had got Pullar for 17 and May for nought, while Hall had bowled Cowdrey for 18.

> *W*es Hall and Chester Watson were bouncing the ball quite alarmingly and Ken Barrington had been hit on the side of the head, which actually made him more determined.
>
> FRED TRUEMAN

Barrington found support in Ted Dexter. They added 142 in the next two-and-a-half hours for the fourth wicket, though not long before the close of the first day Dexter fell to the new cap, the local slow left armer, Charran Singh, caught and bowled for 77. M J K Smith now joined Barrington and they started the second day at 220 for four. As he had in Barbados, Barrington, relishing the challenge, went on to his hundred, eventually caught behind off Hall for 121 after the pair had

added 77 for the fifth wicket. It was 276 for five, but Smith guided the rest of the England batting to add another 106 runs, reaching his own century on the way, before he was eventually ninth out, to Ramadhin, for 108.

Joe Solomon takes evasive action as Trueman whips up a storm in Kingston

It was a hard-baked sort of wicket one came across in the West Indies. It had even bounce, but a bit of pace in it to help the bowlers.

FRED TRUEMAN

The West Indies had to bat for just under half an hour on the second day, an awkward period, particularly in the face of an England total of 382. Both Trueman and Statham made it more so. Trueman was warned for overdoing the bouncers, as Watson and Hall had been earlier.

It wasn't so good, this bouncer business with Hall and Watson. There was talk in the dressing room about retaliation and unfortunately I flattened Conrad Hunte with a bouncer. That put a stop to it, actually. It cooled down, because I think one or two of the West Indies batsmen said to their bowlers, 'Just cut it down a bit, because they've got a couple that can do it as well.' And after that we had a very friendly series.

FRED TRUEMAN

Test Match Special

Hunte and Solomon survived the onslaught that evening, but the next day Trueman and Statham started to run through them. Statham had Hunte caught at leg slip for 8, and then Trueman had Kanhai for 5, Sobers for 0 and Worrell for 9, and when Butcher was lbw to Statham for 9, it was 45 for five. Joe Solomon was run out for 23 and Alexander then fell to Trueman for 28. It was now 94 for seven, but the fall of the next wicket led to trouble beyond a batting collapse.

It all started right at the start of the West Indies innings, when I caught Conrad Hunte off Brian Statham's bowling at leg-slip and he more or less indicated that he hadn't hit the ball. It had come off the bat onto his thigh. But the crowd started to simmer from that moment onwards and of course as the West Indies wickets began to go down it all really built up into a crescendo, which it reached when the boy Singh was run out. Singh was run out by yards and the bottles started coming onto the ground, because there was no doubt about it, the West Indies were going to have to follow on.

FRED TRUEMAN

Trouble erupted on the run out of West Indies' Charran Singh. Bottles were thrown as here Ted Dexter is escorted by police from the field of play

*T*here was a huge crowd, probably over 30,000. It was very hot, the rum was flowing and the West Indies were being humiliated by Statham and Trueman who were both bowling at their best.

REX ALSTON

*T*here were some amusing incidents and also some ugly scenes when the bottles and the riot started. The commentary box came under siege as Jeffrey Stollmeyer was commentating and saying it was disgraceful, so they turned their full fury on the commentary box. I said to Brian Statham, 'Grab a stump and we'll protect ourselves on the way off the ground.' We were making our way back to the pavilion when one of the crowd said to me, 'Don't you worry man, it's the umpires we want.' And the umpire who had given the run out was a man called Lee Kow, who was possibly the best umpire that I had played under abroad.

We were sitting in the pavilion waiting and we saw a man starting to collect bottles and we thought, 'There's a man with a bit of sense'. And he suddenly started skimming these bottles left-handed back into the crowd just above the fence with magnificent accuracy. He cleared this stand within a matter of minutes.

When the riot squad arrived they laid a hosepipe onto the field and the pump started up and you could see the bulge of water going down the pipe and a man at the nozzle end was standing ready to shower the crowd when it burst right behind him and the fountain of water went right up his backside and the crowd fell about laughing.

FRED TRUEMAN

*A*t no time did I fear for my safety but I was extremely concerned about my wife Elspeth, who was watching the game with friends in the grandstand. I rushed over dramatically to 'save' my better half and found her standing high on a seat, smiling broadly. 'This is the most exciting day's cricket I have ever seen,' she said, 'We must come to the West Indies more often, dear!'

REX ALSTON

Umpire Eric Lee Kow was put under armed police guard after his controversial run-out decision during West Indies first innings

The riot brought a premature end to the third day's play and there was a rest day, by happy chance, before the fourth day, which was thus able to start in a calmer atmosphere, even though Trueman and Statham took little time to polish off the innings for 112. Perhaps because these were six-day Tests — albeit with shorter hours of play — May did not enforce the follow-on and England, again most troubled by Hall and Watson, were able to declare, after a rapid eighth wicket stand of 68 between Illingworth and Trueman, at 230 for nine, setting the West Indies a target of 501 in ten hours.

West Indies' only real chance was to bat out the two days, and they ended the fifth day at 134 for two with Allen having removed both openers, caught behind. Rohan Kanhai was there with Sobers, so all was not lost for the home side. But on the final day, though Kanhai batted on for a fine hundred, no one stayed with him.

> *When they talk about the West Indies' great players, Kanhai's name doesn't seem to get mentioned too much, but I always think he was one of the most underrated players. He was a very fine player, with a keen eye.*
>
> FRED TRUEMAN

The closing stages of the match were marred by May's refusal of a runner for Kanhai after the latter had developed leg trouble. May apologised later and explained that he had misinterpreted the law. Kanhai was out for 110 and England won by 256 runs with the best part of two hours to spare.

May's uncharacteristic rejection of Kanhai's request for a runner might be explained by the fact that he was himself suffering from an illness which was not discovered until the next Test. Specialist advice forced his return to England, and Cowdrey took over the captaincy. Cowdrey had made 114 and 97 in that drawn Test in Jamaica, with Sobers making a hundred. In addition, Sobers, Raman Subba Row and Dexter all made centuries in the drawn Test in British Guiana. So the series hung on the final Test back in Trinidad, where not only did Cowdrey make another hundred and Sobers 92, but Jim Parks — not part of the original team, but who had been brought into the party as he was coaching there — made a match-saving century in the second innings. England had won a series in the Caribbean for the first time.

Ken Barrington completed his second successive century on tour

FINAL · SCORES

ENGLAND - First Innings

G Pullar, c Alexander b Watson	17
M C Cowdrey, b Hall	18
K F Barrington, c Alexander b Hall	121
P B H May, c Kanhai b Watson	0
E R Dexter, c and b Singh	77
M J K Smith, c Worrell b Ramadhin	108
R Illingworth, b Ramadhin	10
R Swetman, lbw b Watson	1
F S Trueman, lbw b Ramadhin	7
D A Allen, not out	10
J B Statham, b Worrell	1
Extras (lb3, w1, nb8)	12
Total	**382**

Fall of wickets: 1-37, 2-42, 3-57, 4-199, 5-276, 6-307, 7-308, 8-343, 9-378
Bowling: Hall 33-9-92-2, Watson 31-5-100-3, Worrell 11.5-3-23-1, Singh 23-6-59-1, Ramadhin 35-12-61-3, Sobers 3-0-16-0, Solomon 7-0-19-0

WEST INDIES - First Innings

C Hunte, c Trueman b Statham	8
J Solomon, run out	23
R Kanhai, lbw b Trueman	5
G Sobers, c Barrington b Trueman	0
F M Worrell, c Swetman b Trueman	9
B Butcher, lbw b Statham	9
F C M Alexander, lbw b Trueman	28
S Ramadhin, b Trueman	23
C Singh, run out	0
W Hall, b Statham	4
C Watson, not out	0
Extras (lb2, w1)	3
Total	**112**

Fall of wickets: 1-22, 2-31, 3-31, 4-45, 5-45, 6-73, 7-94, 8-98, 9-108
Bowling: Trueman 21-11-35-5, Statham 19.3-8-42-3, Allen 5-0-9-0, Barrington 16-10-15-0, Illingworth 7-3-8-0

ENGLAND - Second Innings

G Pullar, c Worrell b Ramadhin	28
M C Cowdrey, c Alexander b Watson	5
K F Barrington, c Alexander b Hall	49
P B H May, c and b Singh	28
E R Dexter, b Hall	0
M J K Smith, lbw b Watson	12
R Illingworth, not out	41
R Swetman, lbw b Singh	0
F S Trueman, c Alexander b Watson	37
D A Allen, c Alexander b Hall	16
Extras (b6, lb2, w4, nb2)	14
Total (9 wkts dec)	**230**

Fall of wickets: 1-18, 2-79, 3-97, 4-101, 5-122, 6-133, 7-133, 8-201, 9-230
Bowling: Hall 23.4-4-50-3, Watson 19-6-57-3, Worrell 12-5-27-0, Singh 8-3-28-2, Ramadhin 28-8-54-1

WEST INDIES - Second Innings

C Hunte, c Swetman b Allen	47
J Solomon, c Swetman b Allen	9
R Kanhai, c Smith b Dexter	110
G Sobers, lbw b Trueman	31
F M Worrell, lbw b Statham	0
B Butcher, lbw b Statham	9
F C M Alexander, c Trueman b Allen	7
S Ramadhin, lbw b Dexter	0
C Singh, c and b Barrington	11
W Hall, not out	0
C Watson, c Allen b Barrington	0
Extras (b11, lb6, w2, nb1)	20
Total	**244**

Fall of wickets: 1-29, 2-107, 3-158, 4-159, 5-188, 6-222, 7-222, 8-244, 9-244
Bowling: Trueman 19-9-44-1, Statham 25-12-44-2, Allen 31-13-57-3, Barrington 25.5-13-34-2, Illingworth 28-14-38-0, Dexter 6-3-7-2

England won by 256 runs

1963 Lord's

SECOND TEST, 20-22, 24, 25 JUNE

Commentators: JOHN ARLOTT, ALAN GIBSON, ROY LAWRENCE
Summarisers: NORMAN YARDLEY

*I*t was a ding-dong struggle: first one side was doing well,
and then the other. It was one of the best matches I have
ever attended.

BRIAN JOHNSTON

This was one of those Test matches that sticks in the memory for those
who followed it on the radio, just as much as for those who were there.
West Indies, under the captaincy of Frank Worrell, had won the first
Test at Old Trafford by ten wickets, having run up 501 for six declared
in their first innings, with Hunte making 182, Kanhai 90 and Sobers 64,
and then, England had been bowled out twice, not so much by the
devastating fast bowling combination of Wes Hall and Charlie Griffith as
by the off-spin of Lance Gibbs, who succeeded in taking eleven wickets
in the match.

For Lord's, England, under Ted Dexter, brought in the veteran Derek
Shackleton to share the new ball with Trueman, and strengthened the
batting by bringing in Jim Parks to keep wicket instead of Keith
Andrew. Worrell won the toss and Conrad Hunte launched the West
Indies innings in sensational fashion with three fours off the first three
balls sent down by Trueman.

*C*onrad Hunte got fourteen runs off me in the first over,
but ten of them went through the slips and nobody laid
a hand on the ball and, of course, bowling as I did then
without a third man, once the ball went through there it was
four runs.

FRED TRUEMAN

Despite that flying start, Hunte and Easton McMorris did not find the
going at all easy, especially as a shower had eaten twenty minutes out of
the morning session, by the end of which they had got the score to 47.
Only four runs had been added in the afternoon when Trueman started
his revenge for earlier indignities, having McMorris lbw for 16 and soon
afterwards dismissing Hunte for 44. Rohan Kanhai and Gary Sobers
added 63 for the third wicket and after Sobers had fallen to David
Allen's off-spin for 42 and Basil Butcher had been caught off Trueman

Conrad Hunte upset Fred Trueman by taking 14 runs from the bowler's first over

T e s t   M a t c h   S p e c i a l

43

Colin Cowdrey dives to his left to pouch a sharp chance from Gary Sobers off David Allen for 42

for 14, Kanhai was joined by Solomon in a fifth wicket stand of 74. As the first day drew to a close, Trueman at last removed Kanhai for 73. But at 219 for five it was a daunting prospect to see the great Frank Worrell coming to the wicket.

REX ALSTON *Now what's Dexter doing, he's moving in from cover point, he's going to post himself at point, just a yard behind point and not more than six yards from the bat. Trueman to Worrell. . .and he's bowled him.*

The scalp of Worrell for a duck before the close was a great fillip to England. However, the West Indies ended the day at 245 for six. England did not have to wait long next day for another success. Murray caught at slip off Trueman for 20 and then at last Shackleton got his deserved reward.

REX ALSTON *Well he's certainly earned a wicket has Shackleton, bowls again to Solomon. . .and he hit him on the pad this time, he's got his wicket, lbw. So in his fiftieth over Shackleton has got the wicket that he has been toiling for since half past eleven yesterday morning. Solomon disappears from my view as he goes up the Pavilion steps and the West Indies are now 297 for eight, Hall not out 21, Solomon leg before wicket to Shackleton for 56.*

Test Match Special

I have never seen a ball move around more and the batsmen play and miss more than on the first morning, when Shackleton was bowling. But he got no wickets. In the end he finished up with three, but he got those on the second day. He absolutely bamboozled the batsmen and bowled marvellously but it was Trueman who picked up the wickets.

BRIAN JOHNSTON

Shackleton cleaned up the tail with figures of three for 93 from 50 overs and two balls. Trueman had bowled 44 overs to take six for 100 and the West Indies were all out for 301.

The formidable Griffith removed the Surrey opening pair of John Edrich and Micky Stewart before lunch on that second day, which brought together the dogged Ken Barrington and Corinthian figure of Dexter at a critical point with England 20 for two. Dexter took on the ferocious pace of Hall and Griffith and through that Friday afternoon answered it with a ferocity of his own.

JOHN ARLOTT *It's Hall to bowl now to Dexter, he comes in from the Nursery end at full split and bowls, and Dexter plays that very calmly back down the pitch off the middle of the bat as if Hall were a medium pacer. There is about Dexter when he chooses to face fast bowling with*

T e s t   M a t c h   S p e c i a l

determination a sort of air of command that lifts him or seems to lift him above ordinary players. He seems to find time to play the fastest of bowling and still retain dignity something near majesty as he does it. In again comes Hall from the Nursery end, bowls to Dexter who gets over it and hooks it imperiously downwards past McMorris up at silly mid-on for two. McMorris turns to the alarm of an otherwise peaceful pigeon and throws back, the pigeon takes off and goes straight into the Pavilion. Still this ominous looking field with the men deep for the nick and up close for the man who plays back so that the ball pops up. Hall comes in, bowls to Dexter who gets over it and hooks it magnificently away there down to mid-wicket. It's chased but fruitlessly by McMorris, it's another four. This takes Dexter up to 33 out of 47. Of course he's made bigger scores than 33 in Test matches and he may well do so this time but I think I've never seen Dexter bat more reassuringly nor more commandingly.

Dexter's innings lasted only 81 minutes and he faced only 73 balls, but he made 70 and those who saw it still recall it vividly.

Dexter's 70 was undoubtedly the best short innings I have ever seen in Test cricket, if you can call 70 short. He attacked the fast bowlers brilliantly, cutting them and forcing them past mid-on and mid-off. It was a really great innings.

BRIAN JOHNSTON

He stood upright in the old amateur cavalier fashion that one had read about and drove Hall and Griffith back past them as they followed through. It was a tremendous innings and anyone who watched it will always remember it. The only sad part was that he didn't go on and make the hundred he deserved. He played majestically and I don't think anyone has ever hit the ball harder.

FRED TRUEMAN

It was Sobers who eventually dismissed Dexter, lbw, after a stand of 82 for the third wicket which had occupied only just over an hour. Barrington had been a minor partner in that partnership, but now he had to take the lead as Colin Cowdrey and Brian Close went cheaply and, at 151 for five, England were still 150 runs behind. With Jim Parks, Barrington shared a sixth wicket stand of 55 at getting on a run a minute, but Frank Worrell ended both innings, Parks bowled for 35 and Barrington caught at cover for 80. A full house on Saturday morning saw England claw their way to within four runs of the West Indies score, largely thanks to a determined 52 not out from Fred Titmus.

This time Shackleton and Trueman quickly disposed of the ·West

Indian openers with only 15 runs on the board. Kanhai was joined by Butcher, who had received a letter that day from his troubled home country of British Guiana informing him that his wife had just had a miscarriage. It was a terrible start to what was to become his day. However, there was more trouble to come before that as Kanhai was caught at slip for 21 off Shackleton, Trueman had Sobers caught behind for 8 and Allen had Solomon caught for 5. West Indies were 104 for five — and only 108 ahead. Now Butcher was joined by his captain and he really began to assert himself, with Worrell playing the supporting role. Before the close of the third day, Butcher reached an impressive century.

ROY LAWRENCE *Shackleton again, these two have added 61 runs, in he comes to bowl to Butcher and Butcher's hit him over the head again and it's going down for four. . .it is, and there's his hundred. What a tremendous ovation.*

Over the Sunday rest day the West Indies stood at 214 for five, in a commanding position with a lead of 218. But on the Monday morning, when the fine weather was looking a little less certain, they dramatically lost those last five wickets for the addition of only 15 runs. Trueman first removed Worrell for 33 and Murray and Hall cheaply, and then Shackleton ended Butcher's great innings, lbw for 133, and bowled Griffith to end the West Indies innings. He had taken four for 72 and Trueman five for 52, the latter having taken eleven wickets in the match. England needed 234 to win.

The game had already had its share of swings of fortune, so it might have been expected that in the face of Hall and Griffith's opening onslaught it would turn again West Indies' way. Hall quickly disposed of Stewart and Edrich and Gibbs bowled Dexter for 2. England were 31 for three. Barrington was joined by Cowdrey, who owed England a few runs. On a gloomy day and in the face of a considerable amount of hostile, fast and short-pitched bowling these two battled their way to a 50 partnership. Then a ball from Hall took off from a reasonably good length and took Cowdrey on the left wrist as he parried it away from his face. Hall later was in no doubt that he had discovered the infamous Lord's 'ridge'. Everyone on the field had heard the loud snap and it was obvious that the wrist was broken. Cowdrey had to retire at 19 and so England were in further trouble. It was 72 for three, effectively for four.

West Indies certainly believed they were on the way to victory now as Brian Close came in to replace Cowdrey. Barrington was at his most defiant, hitting Gibbs twice in one over for six over mid-wicket.

Barrington played a wonderful innings and made a lot of runs very quickly on the fourth evening, playing some lovely attacking shots, to put England well ahead of the

Test Match Special

clock. But Barrington went right into his shell after the rain on the final day, and it became obvious that England were going to be pushed for time with the bowling rate at only fourteen overs an hour.

BRIAN JOHNSTON

The weather was now taking a hand in the course of the match. It had ended play shortly after tea on the fourth day with England 116 for three, not quite half way to their target. It now delayed the start of the final day until lunch. In 55 minutes, Barrington added only five to his overnight 55, before Griffith had him caught behind and it was 130 for four. Parks also went before tea, lbw to Griffith for 17 and, at that last interval, it was 171 for five. A further 63 runs were needed.

Close was playing an innings of rare bravery, so far mostly in defence against the fast bowlers, though after tea he decided that more aggression was needed.

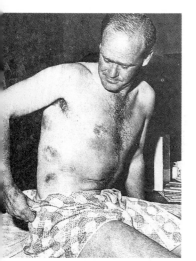

Brian Close displays the price he paid for an innings of rare bravery against fearsome pace bowling

That was an innings of great courage beyond what one could expect of someone. He just took full force of Hall and Griffith bowling short on his body and never flinched. In fact he was delighted next day to have his photograph taken showing his bruised body looking like a leopard. It was an innings deserving victory.

FRED TRUEMAN

The over rate fell. Hall removed Titmus and Trueman, but the target crept closer, with Close now batting with David Allen, with whom he added 16.

ROY LAWRENCE *England now 15 runs wanted for victory and of course Close to face. Close on 70, Allen on two. And that field drops out again, here comes Griffith to bowl to Close, he bowls to him, Close swings at it — there's an appeal for a catch behind the wicket and Close is out. Oh my goodness we are getting everything here now. Close has been caught by Murray off Griffith's bowling and England 219 for eight, still require 15 runs to win. It's no doubt going to be Shackleton to come in and Norman, I think you take some of the pressure off me now.*

NORMAN YARDLEY *Well I certainly think that Close must consider this one of his finest hours and now, what is it, 15 runs to get, two wickets to fall if Cowdrey is going to bat, which we yet don't know. What are these two remaining England batsman going to do?*

There were 19 minutes to go as Shackleton joined Allen. They added another seven runs before Wes Hall came up to bowl the final over.

Test Match Special

*I*t was dramatic from our point of view on the television, because the last over was just about to begin when the producer suddenly said: 'Right, got to get back to Alexandra Palace for the news.' I was flabbergasted that we were going to miss the finish, but half way through a report on President Kennedy, the newsreader suddenly said: 'And back to Lord's.' I think we only missed one ball at most.

Wes Hall bowled unchanged all that final afternoon, including the dramatic final over

Test Match Special

Apparently Kenneth Adam, the head of television, was a cricket fan and immediately phoned up and told them to get back to the cricket. So we caught this final over.
BRIAN JOHNSTON

ALAN GIBSON *Here comes Hall bowling to Shackleton. Eight runs needed, last over coming up. Hall bowls and Shackleton swings and it goes through to the wicket-keeper. Worrell is moving an extra man over to the leg side, Hall has only got one slip near the bat now, all the rest scattered and Hall back at the end of his run, 226 for eight, five balls to go, eight runs needed. Hall bowls to Shackleton and they go for a very quick single as he plays it about five yards down the pitch. Hall follows through, tries to throw the wicket down, almost falls flat on his face, but they're through for the run, 227 for eight. Shackleton now goes on to four, overtaking Allen. Allen is three, seven runs are needed for an England victory, two wickets to fall, four balls left. And Hall bowling out of the background of the dark Pavilion on a dark and gloomy evening and after his little bit of excitement there when he followed up and nearly fell over himself he's looking understandably very weary indeed as he trudges back to his mark. A tremendous feat of fast bowling this by Hall and if the West Indies don't win it seems sad that such an almost super-human effort of valour should not have been in a winning cause. Four balls to go, Hall comes in, bowling to Allen, bowls to him and Allen plays that down to long leg there's one more run there. 228 for eight, Allen goes on to four, six runs are needed and three balls are left as Shackleton has the bowling. A feverish atmosphere now as Hall comes in with three balls to go and bowls to Shackleton and Shackleton flashes outside the off-stump, doesn't get a touch and they go through for a very quick single and Shackleton's going to be run out, he's run out, he started off late, Allen ran and got there in fact by following up very quickly but Shackleton was slow to start, they threw it to the bowler's end, the bails were whipped off, Shackleton was well out. 228 for nine, they are not coming in, we must therefore presume that with two balls to go Cowdrey will come in but Allen, as a result of the batsmen having crossed, has at least got the bowling so Cowdrey may not have to face a ball. And the applause seems to me to indicate that Cowdrey is coming out and the cheering tells you that in fact he is. There are two balls to go, England, needing 234 to win are 228 for nine, with Cowdrey, his left forearm in plaster, coming out to join Allen. Cowdrey is of course 19 already, having retired hurt and the crowd now swarming out of the stands, coming up, the West Indians particularly, coming up eagerly right around the boundary rope waiting to charge on to the field as soon as this dramatic and gripping Test match has ended. And end it is bound to either in the next ball or the one after that because there are only the two left, six runs wanted to win. Here comes the first of them, Hall bowling to Allen, bowls to him and Allen plays it out on the off-side and there is no run, and*

With two balls remaining and six runs required for an England win, last man Colin Cowdrey walks out to resume his innings with a broken wrist

therefore with one ball left to go, barring any accidents like no ball, and I wouldn't put that beyond us, this game has had a surprise for us at every stage of its course. And Wesley Hall is going to bowl the last ball of the match from the Pavilion end to Allen. He comes in and bowls it and Allen plays defensively and the match is drawn and the crowd come swarming onto the field, Cowdrey does not have to play a ball, the ground staff, the policemen are desperately rushing out to protect the sacred middle. The West Indies cricketers being chased in by their own enthusiastic supporters. Wesley Hall, still with a tremendous run in him, leading the rush off the field. The end of a great game of cricket.

After a game like that, let nobody doubt that a draw really can be as exciting as any other result.

Test Match Special

The end of an exciting
five days of cricket.
Cowdrey and David
Allen run for the shelter
of the pavilion, the
match saved

FINAL · SCORES

WEST INDIES - First Innings

C C Hunte, c Close b Trueman	44
E D McMorris, lbw b Trueman	16
G S Sobers, c Cowdrey b Allen	42
R B Kanhai, c Edrich b Trueman	73
B F Butcher, c Barrington b Trueman	14
J S Solomon, lbw b Shackleton	56
F M Worrell, b Trueman	0
D L Murray, c Cowdrey b Trueman	20
W W Hall, not out	25
C C Griffith, c Cowdrey b Shackleton	0
L R Gibbs, c Stewart b Shackleton	0
Extras (b10, lb1)	11
Total	301

Fall of wickets: 1-51, 2-64, 3-127, 4-145, 5-219, 6-219, 7-263, 8-297, 9-297
Bowling: Trueman 44-16-100-6, Shackleton 50.2-22-93-3, Dexter 20-6-41-0, Close 9-3-21-0, Allen 10-3-35-1

ENGLAND - First Innings

M J Stewart, c Kanhai b Griffith	2
J H Edrich, c Murray b Griffith	0
E R Dexter, lbw b Sobers	70
K F Barrington, c Sobers b Worrell	80
M C Cowdrey, b Gibbs	4
D B Close, c Murray b Griffith	9
J M Parks, b Worrell	35
F J Titmus, not out	52
F S Trueman, b Hall	10
D A Allen, lbw b Griffith	2
D Shackleton, b Griffith	8
Extras (b8, lb8, nb9)	25
Total	297

Fall of wickets: 1-2, 2-20, 3-102, 4-115, 5-151, 6-206, 7-235, 8-271, 9-274
Bowling: Hall 18-2-65-1, Griffith 26-6-91-5, Sobers 18-4-45-1, Gibbs 27-9-59-1, Worrell 13-6-12-2

WEST INDIES - Second Innings

C C Hunte, c Cowdrey b Shackleton	7
E D McMorris, c Cowdrey b Trueman	8
G S Sobers, c Parks b Trueman	8
R B Kanhai, c Cowdrey b Shackleton	21
B F Butcher, lbw b Shackleton	133
J S Solomon, c Stewart b Allen	5
F M Worrell, c Stewart b Trueman	33
D L Murray, c Parks b Trueman	2
W W Hall, c Parks b Trueman	2
C C Griffith, b Shackleton	1
L R Gibbs, not out	1
Extras (b5, lb2, nb1)	8
Total	229

Fall of wickets: 1-15, 2-15, 3-64, 4-84, 5-104, 6-214, 7-224, 8-226, 9-228
Bowling: Trueman 26-9-52-5, Shackleton 34-14-72-4, Titmus 17-3-47-0, Allen 21-7-50-1

ENGLAND - Second Innings

M J Stewart, c Solomon b Hall	17
J H Edrich, c Murray b Hall	8
E R Dexter, b Gibbs	2
K F Barrington, c Murray b Griffith	60
M C Cowdrey, not out	19
D B Close, c Murray b Griffith	70
J M Parks, lbw b Griffith	17
F J Titmus, c McMorris b Hall	11
F S Trueman, c Murray b Hall	0
D A Allen, not out	4
D Shackleton, run out	4
Extras (b5, lb8, nb3)	16
Total (9 wkts)	228

Fall of wickets: 1-15, 2-27, 3-31, 4-130, 5-158, 6-203, 7-203, 8-219, 9-228
Bowling: Hall 40-9-93-4, Griffith 30-7-59-3, Sobers 4-1-4-0, Gibbs 17-7-56-1,

Match drawn

1966 The Oval

FIFTH TEST, 18-20, 22 AUGUST

Commentators: JOHN ARLOTT, ROY LAWRENCE, ROBERT HUDSON
Summarisers: FREDDIE BROWN

The year 1966 is probably best remembered in English sporting history as the year Alf Ramsey's lads won the World Cup at Wembley. However, while they were doing that, Gary Sobers' powerful and experienced West Indies had taken a winning 3-0 lead in the Test series and England had sacked two captains. The first was M J K Smith, who had taken the side to Australia the previous winter, failing to regain the Ashes in a drawn series. At Old Trafford, where the West Indies had won by an innings with centuries from Hunte and Sobers, Smith had provided Lance Gibbs with two of his ten wickets. He was replaced for the next Test by Colin Cowdrey, who led England to what looked like the verge of victory at Lord's, only for Sobers and his young cousin, David Holford, who was playing in only his second Test, to save the game with a hundred apiece. At Trent Bridge, West Indies came back from a ninety-run first innings deficit with a double century from Basil Butcher to win by 139 runs and, at Headingley, centuries from Nurse and Sobers, the bowling of Sobers — again — and Gibbs took them to another innings victory and the certainty of winning the series.

So the England selectors wielded the axe. Six changes were made to the side for the Oval Test. Out went Colin Milburn, Jim Parks, Fred Titmus and Derek Underwood to be replaced by the new cap Dennis Amiss, John Edrich, John Murray to keep wicket and Ray Illingworth. Originally, too, John Snow was dropped, but he was recalled when his replacement, John Price, had to withdraw. The captain, Cowdrey, gave way to Yorkshire's captain, Brian Close.

Sobers won the toss and decided to bat. John Snow opened the bowling from the Vauxhall end, conceding just a single to Hunte, who now prepared to face Ken Higgs bowling the second over of the match from the Pavilion End.

ROY LAWRENCE *D'Oliveira and Graveney in the slips, Illingworth in the gully, Amiss in the covers. There's no mid-off. Close very near to the bat at forward short leg and Edrich is at mid on. Barber at leg slip and Snow down on the long leg boundary. Higgs now in from the Pavilion End, he bowls to Hunte and he's bowled him. Knocked the middle stick out of the ground. And that gives Higgs his 50th wicket in Test cricket. Hunte, bowled Higgs for one.*

West Indies supporters
in bouyant mood at
Old Trafford, where
their team won by an
innings

The wicket of Hunte was just the start of a good morning for England as Snow bowled the other opener, McMorris, for 14. Close got Basil Butcher for 12 and Basil D'Oliveira removed Seymour Nurse for a duck. It was 74 for four when Sobers, shortly before lunch joined Rohan Kanhai. The afternoon was to belong to them as, with masterful strokeplay, they built up a partnership of 122.

JOHN ARLOTT *Snow to Kanhai, and he drives him, through mid-on, over the top of mid-on, four runs. Kanhai 99. That ball was well up to him and he pull-drove it, lofted it. Not afraid to chance his arm and it's Snow now to Kanhai again. In. Bowls. Kanhai pushes that half way up the wicket, wants a quick single. Sobers sends him back and makes little soothing motions with his hand to Kanhai as if to say there, there we've got all the week. He's not a man as a general rule over afflicted with patience when it comes to batting. Snow comes in, bowls to him and he goes onto the back foot, forces, beats Graveney and there's his hundred. That's four. A lovely back foot force and the pitch invaded by West Indians and not all West*

Rohan Kanhai pulls to the boundary on his way to 104 out of a West Indies total of 268

Indians either, though mainly I should think a good Caribbean majority. There must be 80 to 100 people on the pitch seeking to shake hands with Kanhai who's fending them off with his bat. 189 for four, Kanhai 103.

Soon after he had reached his hundred, Kanhai was caught by Graveney as he swept at Illingworth for 104. That precipitated something of a collapse as Bob Barber, with his leg-spin, picked up Sobers, caught at straight mid-wicket for 81, and also removed Jackie Hendriks and Charlie Griffith cheaply and Illingworth had Holford for 5. However, Wes Hall and Gibbs managed a face-saving last wicket stand of 45. The West Indies had been bowled out in the day for 268. There was still time on that first day for England to lose Geoff Boycott, bowled by Hall for 4, so Barber and Edrich started the second day taking their partnership to 66. The introduction of Sobers, bowling his slow left-arm variety brought the demise of Barber for 36 and then Edrich for 35 before Dennis Amiss arrived at the crease.

ROY LAWRENCE *These two have taken the England total from 85 for three to 126 for three. Hall back at his mark now and turns, runs in now to bowl to Amiss. Amiss on 17. Hall is up, he bowls to Amiss and hits him on the pad and he's out lbw. As plumb as anyone could be I'd have said. Freddie that cut back and hit him right in the middle.*
FREDDIE BROWN *Yes it was a very good ball. It came back at him very late. Kept a little bit low I think but Amiss was in completely the wrong position and I don't think umpire Buller had any doubt about it at all.*
ROY LAWRENCE *And in our position here we're absolutely right over the two stumps and he looked plumb out.*

Hall followed the wicket of Amiss by bowling D'Oliveira for 4. Five wickets down and after lunch the new captain had a considerable responsibility on his shoulders.

ROBERT HUDSON *And I should think a good many of this big crowd, there must be well over 25,000 if they've shut the gates I imagine, will be wanting Brian Close to do well in this his first Test as captain. He's come through the first period of the match with flying colours. He captained the side exceedingly well in the field. Now comes the ordeal of his first innings as captain in a difficult situation or rather a tricky situation for England with the game very much in the balance. Here's Hall into Close. It's a full pitch and it's down into the gully, a beautiful throw in and he's out. Close is given run out by umpire Buller. A magnificent throw by Holford from the gully as Close played that one hard into the gully, Holford scooped it up and in one motion hurled the ball at the wicket, hit it and, as I read it Norman, Brian Close just hadn't got his bat down in time.*

Close was run out for 4 and only another 16 runs came before Illingworth was caught behind off Griffith for 3. At 166 for seven, John Murray came in to join Tom Graveney. To his first ball he got the faintest of inside edges onto his pad to survive a fervent shout for lbw and after that he was away. So confidently did he bat, indeed, that Tom Graveney felt no need to farm the strike. the runs mounted as Graveney began to play his shots and the pair found themselves breaking the eighth wicket record against West Indies.

JOHN ARLOTT *Sobers takes another look at the field. Murray quite gently tapping, checks up, cuts. There they go they've got their one. They've broken the record. 96 now — a record that's stood for 33 years. Let's watch Sobers now bowl to Graveney. In, bowls to him, pitched up, Graveney swings it over leg side. It's four runs. He's there. He's got his hundred. A* *flock of little boys tearing onto the ground. This won't do at all. Oh no. Oh no. Batsmen fending them off, and umpires. There must be 200 of them. This will not do. Oh no! They've even wrecked the stumps. The West Indians applauding the innings. I'm bound to point out that that was a full toss from Sobers which Graveney swung for four and here come the drinks. Let us say that in a day when many people think the rest of the England batting failed there was this man, the senior of them all, demonstrating that it wasn't quite so difficult as some people might make it look. It becomes tragic now that he's been out of Test cricket for so long. It's said, alright he's 39, he can't last long but Jack Hobbs made over a hundred centuries after he was*

Tom Graveney attempts to turn the tide of invading schoolboys after reaching his 100

40 and this man has something of the same ease as Jack Hobbs. Something of the rightness about when to go forward and when to go back. A fine forward player who makes superb strokes off the back foot and today he's done himself credit and he's done English cricket I think great credit in withstanding some extremely skillful bowling and some very artful tactics.

At the close of the second day England, from the unpromising position in which the partnership had started, had actually taken a lead of 62 at 330 for seven. On Saturday morning Murray resumed, just nineteen runs short of his century in this, his first Test against the West Indies.

JOHN ARLOTT *Now then Griffith to Murray. Murray 97 and Griffith from the Pavilion end moves in, bowls to him, and he whips that off his pads. This is going to be it. This is going to be it. It's being chased by Holford...2, 3, there's his hundred. And getting as much applause from the West Indian spectators as from the English, and from every West Indian player except Griffith. And Griffith comes up again from the Pavilion end, and bowls to Graveney, a slower ball and my goodness, what a good ball, oh he's run out. No he isn't. . . He's out, Graveney's out. Graveney set off for a run. Murray sent him back. Lance Gibbs moving at immense speed ran with the ball and ran three times as fast as Graveney and broke the stumps. A superb run out. Three eighty-three for eight but what a sad way for the partnership to end.*

Tom Graveney made 96 at Lord's on his return to Test cricket, and then he played this marvellous innings at the Oval. He was aged 39 and an absolute joy to watch. It didn't matter whether he was defending or attacking, everything was so fluent and elegant.

John Murray, JT, was a really good batsman who could very nearly have been in the England team for his batting alone.

BRIAN JOHNSTON

So Graveney was run out for 165, but that partnership had added 217 and had transformed the game. If England were not totally in command, at least they had a substantial lead of 115. The command was to come from an unlikely source. Murray was lbw to Sobers for 112 and, with Snow joining Higgs the end was surely near. It was Saturday morning, and the weary Graveney asked his number eleven batsman if he could possibly contrive to give him a bit more recovery time by hanging on to lunchtime. He did more than that.

ROBERT HUDSON *Here comes Hunte, bowls to Snow. He turns him on the leg-side, square. That's his 50. He's going back for the second run, 50 for*

Snow. And with one deft push on the leg side for two he gets his 50 and puts up the hundred partnership for the last wicket. It is almost incredible. Here is Griffith up to Higgs. He drives it on the off side. That's one. It might or might not be. . .yes it's the 50 for Higgs. Well that's 50 to Ken Higgs and apparently that fulfils a prediction because he said last night apparently to Bill Frindall that he would get 50 today and it was jolly hard luck he only got 49 at Leeds so he's done it. Good luck to Higgs and a very fine effort indeed. 501 for nine.

JOHN ARLOTT *Six saving the one and only one man near to the stumps and Higgs and Snow two runs short of the Test last wicket record and Holford bowls to Higgs, pitches up and Higgs drives this back to him and he's out, caught and bowled Holford. Higgs caught and bowled Holford 63. John Snow not out 59 and a hundred and twenty-eight for the last wicket.*

*T*here was a fantastic partnership between Snow and Higgs in which they each scored their maiden half-centuries in first-class cricket. The West Indies were hammering to get them out and they faced all the bowlers. It was lovely to watch them, and by the smiles on their faces it gave them so much pleasure.

BRIAN JOHNSTON

Higgs and Snow in that last wicket stand of 128 may have missed the Test tenth wicket record, but it was the first time that the last three wickets in a Test innings had amassed as many as 361 runs and that the last three men had made a century and two fifties. Now England really had taken command, with a lead of 259.

The West Indies started their second innings after tea on the third day with two full days and that session stretching ahead of them. Snow immediately increased their woes by having both openers caught behind with only 12 runs on the board. With the score on 50, D'Oliveira bowled Kanhai for 15. It seemed that there would be no further alarm that evening, but just before the close Butcher was caught at mid-wicket off a full toss from Illingworth for a defiant 60. It was 135 for four at the close. Sobers had been saved for Monday morning, with Holford going in ahead of him.

The next breakthrough came in the second over of that fourth day.

ROY LAWRENCE *Holford on five, Nurse on 41. And Snow coming in from the Vauxhall end to bowl to Holford. Up he comes. He bowls to Holford. Holford plays him into the slips there all along the ground, Illingworth misfields at gully and they run one, they run two. Illingworth got a hand to it and Holford wants a third but he better get back. He's out! He's run out. Holford has been run out. Oh my goodness what a shock for the West Indies. A good return from Ray Illingworth. I don't know where Holford*

Brian Close (centre) leaves the field after the match. It was his catch to dismiss Sobers that effectively clinched the game for England

thought he was going after his second run, Norman Yardley, but he didn't have time to get back on account of that magnificent throw in from Ray Illingworth. So Holford run out for seven and the West Indies now 137 for five.

As Holford departed for the Pavilion and his cousin, Sobers, started that familiar loose-limbed amble to the wicket, the England fielders gathered and it was decided that Snow should bang the first ball in short to the West Indies captain.

ROY LAWRENCE *Here comes Snow now in to bowl to Sobers and Sobers hits it. He's out. He's caught by Close first ball at forward short leg. Oh well that put paid, I should think, to the West Indies.*

Who else would have been in there at short-leg but the new England captain himself, Brian Close? Sobers believed that any other fielder would have flinched at the hook shot. That, effectively, had won the match for England. Higgs bowled Hendriks for nought, there was some resistance from the tail, but eventually it was Barber who sealed it.

ROY LAWRENCE *Barber in to bowl to Gibbs and Gibbs is down the wicket and he's out caught and bowled and England have won the Test. Congratulations England. Brian Close congratulating Gibbs who put out his arm there to him and the crowd running on to the field and Griffith being congratulated on by one West Indian there who raced up to him. But this new look England side have won the Test. West Indies are all out for 225 and I think it's full marks to England for turning back this West Indies side in this fifth and final Test by an innings and 34 runs.*

T e s t   M a t c h   S p e c i a l

FINAL · SCORES

WEST INDIES - First Innings

C C Hunt, b Higgs	1
E D A St J McMorris, b Snow	14
R B Kanhai, c Graveney b Illingworth	104
B F Butcher, c Illingworth b Close	12
S M Nurse, c Graveney b D'Oliveira	0
G St A Sobers, c Graveney b Barber	81
D A J Holford, c D'Oliveira b Illingworth	5
J L Hendriks, b Barber	0
C C Griffith, c Higgs b Barber	4
W W Hall, not out	30
L R Gibbs, c Murray b Snow	12
Extras (b1, lb3, nb1)	5
Total	268

Fall of wickets: 1-1, 2-56, 3-73, 4-74, 5-196, 6-218, 7-218, 8-223, 9-223
Bowling: Snow 20.5-1-66-2, Higgs 17-4-52-1, D'Oliveira 21-7-35-1, Close 9-2-21-1, Barber 15-3-49-3, Illingworth 15-7-40-2

ENGLAND - First Innings

G Boycott, b Hall	4
R W Barber, b Nurse b Sobers	36
J H Edrich, c Hendriks b Sobers	35
T W Graveney, run out	165
D L Amiss, lbw b Hall	17
B L D'Oliveira, b Hall	4
D B Close, run out	4
R Illingworth, c Hendriks b Griffith	3
J T Murray, lbw b Sobers	112
K Higgs, c and b Holford	63
J A Snow, not out	59
Extras (b8, lb14, nb3)	25
Total	561

Fall of wickets: 1-6, 2-72, 3-85, 4-126, 5-130, 6-150, 7-166, 8-383, 9-399
Bowling: Hall 31-8-85-3, Griffith 32-7-78-1, Sobers 54-23-104-3, Holford 25.5-1-79-1, Gibbs 44-16-115-0, Hunte 13-2-41-0

WEST INDIES - Second Innings

C C Hunt, b Murray b Snow	7
E D A St J McMorris, c Murray b Snow	1
R B Kanhai, b D'Oliveira	15
B F Butcher, c Barber b Illingworth	60
S M Nurse, c Edrich b Barber	70
D A J Holford, run out	7
G St A Sobers, c Close b Snow	0
J L Hendriks, b Higgs	0
C C Griffith, not out	29
W W Hall, c D'Oliveira b Illingworth	17
L R Gibbs, c and b Barber	3
Extras (b1, lb14, nb1)	16
Total	225

Fall of wickets: 1-5 2-12, 3-50, 4-107, 5-137, 6-137, 7-142, 8-168, 9-204
Bowling: Snow 13-5-40-3, Higgs 15-6-18-1, D'Oliveira 17-4-44-1, Close 3-1-7-0, Barber 22.1-2-78-2, Illingworth 15-9-22-2

England won by an innings and 68 runs

Graveney and John Murray are applauded from the field by the West Indies team during their stand of 217

1968 Queen's Park Oval

FOURTH TEST, 14-16, 18, 19 MARCH

Commentator: BRIAN JOHNSTON

Opposing captains Colin Cowdrey and Gary Sobers flank Dr Eric Williams, Prime Minister of Trinidad and Tobago, in Port-of-Spain

Such have been the economics of tours of the Caribbean that this MCC visit in early 1968 was their first for eight years. Amid considerable controversy over time-wasting tactics in a county match, Brian Close had been relieved of the captaincy and Colin Cowdrey had taken over. He had a strong looking team in support, with Geoff Boycott, John Edrich, Ken Barrington, Tom Graveney, Jim Parks and Basil D'Oliveira in the batting line-up; John Snow, David Brown, Ken Higgs and Jeff Jones as the fast bowlers; and Fred Titmus, Tony Lock, Pat Pocock and Robin Hobbs to spin the ball.

West Indies were still led by Gary Sobers. Basil Butcher, Rohan Kanhai and Seymour Nurse were among the batsmen along with a young man who had started his Test career in India a year before, Clive Lloyd.

Despite an attack that included Wes Hall, Charlie Griffith and Lance Gibbs, England ran up a total of 568 in the drawn first Test in Trinidad, with centuries from Barrington and Graveney It was a draw, too, in Jamaica, where Cowdrey made a hundred and Edrich fell four runs short of one. Snow, after missing the First Test, took seven wickets in West Indies' first innings.

West Indies really wriggled out of defeat in the first two Test matches — in Trinidad, when Gary Sobers and Wes Hall hung on on the last day; and in Jamaica, when they really were up against it and the crowd reacted very violently when a clear decision was given down the leg-side. There was a riot and the match was interrupted. And then Sobers played an unforgettable century.

TONY COZIER

West Indies had followed on in Jamaica, but in the end it was England who found themselves struggling in the extra time added on to compensate for the riot. At the end of the additional hour-and-a-quarter on the sixth morning they were 68 for eight.

The England batsmen continued their first innings form in Barbados, where this time it was Edrich who reached three figures and Boycott got into the nineties. But here, too, despite more wickets for Snow and a first innings lead of a hundred, England could not force a win. Lloyd made his second century of the series to underline his arrival on the international scene.

And so back to Trinidad and the Queen's Park Oval, where the West Indies selectors decided to drop Hall to include the leg-spinner, Willie Rodriguez. With Titmus having left the tour after losing four toes in a painful swimming accident involving a boat's propeller, England played only one specialist spinner, the veteran Tony Lock.

West Indies batted first on a rain-affected day, with Steve

Steve Camacho sweeps Tony Lock during his 87 while Alan Knott and Colin Cowdrey look on

T e s t   M a t c h   S p e c i a l

Camacho, later to become secretary of the West Indies Cricket Board, uncharacteristically dominating an opening stand of 119 with 'Joey' Carew. Brown eventually got them both — Camacho for 87 and Carew for 36, but their efforts were merely a prelude to a partnership which blossomed on the second day between Nurse and Kanhai. In five hours of batting together they added 273 for the third wicket. Kanhai was the more aggressive, making 153. Lock, who had a great deal of work to do, was rewarded with his wicket, while Barrington's occasional leg-spin eventually accounted for Nurse for 136. But by the time they were separated, the West Indies already had a daunting score of 415. The fifth wicket pair of Lloyd and Sobers rammed home the advantage with a partnership of 85, which took that total past 500, Lloyd making 43 and his captain 48. Sobers did not prolong the innings much further, declaring at 526 for seven towards the end of the second day.

England would now be battling to save the game and they started in encouraging fashion.

*B*oycott and Cowdrey had been in tremendous form on the tour and both batted very well in the first innings. If you ever saw Boycott play abroad, you would have to say that he was a very different player from the one he was at home.

BRIAN JOHNSTON

Rohan Kanhai drives majestically for four as Knott and Cowdrey await slim pickings

After Edrich had made 32 out of the first wicket stand of 86, Boycott went on to make 62. The third day ended with England 204 for two. Griffith, who had shared the new ball with Sobers, had to limp off after three overs that morning, which was a serious depletion of the attack, but on the fourth day it looked as if spin would be decisive anyway. Gibbs' off-spin had Barrington lbw for 48 and then Rodriguez's leg-spin had Graveney caught behind for eight and bowled D'Oliveira for a duck. It was 260 for five, but Cowdrey was still there and he was joined now by Alan Knott in a vital stand of 113.

The final turn in the innings came with the introduction of the very occasional leg-spin of Basil Butcher. He may have been a little lucky to be given the wicket of Cowdrey caught behind for 148, but he quickly added to it by bowling Snow for nought and having Brown caught behind for another duck. Lock was his fourth victim, lbw for 3 and at 381 for nine, Knott decided to gather a few last-ditch runs which took his score to 69 before Jeff Jones was at last bowled by Butcher for 1 and England were all out for 414, a deficit of 112. Basil Butcher had taken his first five Test wickets — five for 15 in a spell of ten overs at the end of the innings.

The West Indies needed now to build quickly on that lead and a positive captain like Sobers would be looking for the chance to set up a win with a declaration.

Sobers was the greatest and one of the nicest cricketers there ever was; you could not meet a better sportsman. He was a pleasant captain who could be over-generous because he obviously enjoyed a game of cricket. I think most West Indian captains have not needed to be tremendous captains. Sobers had all these marvellous batsmen, as well as Gibbs, Hall, Griffith and himself, which made the job that much easier.

BRIAN JOHNSTON

Sobers' ambitions for the final day of the match were in danger of being thwarted by England slowing down the game. After an opening stand of 66, Camacho went for 31 and Nurse run out for 9. Carew was 40 not out when his captain took everyone by surprise by declaring at 92 for two.

Sobers felt that that really was not the way that cricket should be played. In fact, England — not uniquely — were just playing for time on the last day. They got through twenty-two overs in the two hours before lunch and at that stage Sobers just seemed to get fed up with the whole thing and he felt, 'Right, let's try to put it over them.' And he took the gamble that he did. He is not one who is averse to having a gamble and he'd got Basil Butcher taking five wickets in the first innings — a freak performance. Perhaps he felt that lightning might strike twice in the same place. It seldom does when that lightning happens to be a very occasional leg-spinner who has never taken a Test wicket before that.

TONY COZIER

It was an extraordinary declaration. Sobers had to rely on his spinners, which was absurd really because they got through so many overs. He couldn't bowl England out in that time, so it was always odds-on that England would win.

BRIAN JOHNSTON

It had been hot and sticky and the declaration had rather taken England by surprise. Certainly their captain, Cowdrey was somewhat suspicious of it, fearing that Sobers was expecting Rodriguez to weave some sort of magic. It is inconceivable that Sobers could have forgotten it, but he was handicapped by the loss of Griffith with his injured leg and probably would have wished that Hall had not been omitted from the side.

It really was a very strange situation in that second innings with Lance Gibbs actually opening the bowling. When you've set a team a target, you want Lance Gibbs to be your off-spinner, not your opening bowler. And when you look at the number of overs that were bowled in that second innings, it wasn't as if the West Indies were able to hold things up by having fast bowlers taking up time.

TONY COZIER

The first nineteen overs saw an opening stand of 55 setting England off on the right course before Rodriguez bowled Edrich for 29. That brought in the more cautious Cowdrey and the progress slowed.

England were going great guns by the tea interval, but Cowdrey was dithering around. The story, and we know it's true, has it that Ken Barrington had to go to him in the loo and say: 'Come on, we can do this, we can do it.' So Colin went out and played some good strokes and Boycott timed it to perfection.

BRIAN JOHNSTON

BRIAN JOHNSTON *Well things have certainly happened since tea. Before tea it looked as if England weren't going to make it, now certainly they stand a very good chance indeed. 46 runs needed, 169 for one, 58 to Boycott, 67 for Cowdrey — one of his great innings. One of his really great innings after tea, he's really been going for it. In comes Gibbs, bowls to Cowdrey again and he hits this one, lobbed this one and it's going to be safe, its going for four I think. . . Charlie Davis can't stop that, that's another four for Cowdrey, his tenth four. They've put on a hundred runs since tea; a hundred in 55 minutes since tea put on by Cowdrey who is now 71 not out, Boycott 58 not out. 42 runs needed. Gibbs bowling to Cowdrey and he hits this one, it's going up in the air, it's going to be caught by Sobers at mid-wicket. Cowdrey is out! Cowdrey's out, caught at mid-wicket, he's out for 71 and already the next batsman is coming out, its Tom Graveney. So England, 173 for two, leaving 42. Cowdrey going for that one, hitting it down to mid-wicket, and the excitement is absolutely tremendous here.*

After Cowdrey had gone, Graveney was bowled by Gibbs for 2, but that second wicket stand between Cowdrey and Boycott had set up England's victory and Boycott now took command and was 80 when the winning run came with three minutes and seven wickets to spare.

Test Match Special

Colin Cowdrey survives an appeal for leg-before during his magnificent 148

*T*o have got themselves into such a strong position and then to have lost on a declaration was something more than West Indians could either accept or bear and following the defeat there were demonstrations in the heart of Port-of-Spain, where Gary Sobers was hung in effigy in Independence Square.

There is a story that when he arrived in Guyana for the final Test, Sobers was asked by the customs officer if he had anything to declare. He replied that he would never declare anything again in his life. Sobers realised that he'd put the West Indies in the position that they were in — one-nil down in the series — and he made a Herculean effort in Guyana almost to win the Test match himself. Even by his standards he put in a really amazing all-round performance.

TONY COZIER

The fifth and final Test ended up in a draw, and thus England clinched the series 1-0.

Test Match Special

FINAL · SCORES

WEST INDIES - First Innings

S Camacho, c Knott b Brown	87
M C Carew, c Lock b Brown	36
S M Nurse, c Edrich b Barrington	136
R B Kanhai, c Barrington b Lock	153
C H Lloyd, b Jones	43
G S Sobers, c Jones b Brown	48
B F Butcher, not out	7
W V Rodriguez, b Jones	0
D L Murray, not out	5
Extras (lb6, nb5)	11
Total (7 wkts dec)	**526**

Fall of wickets: 1-119, 2-142, 3-415, 4-421, 5-506, 6-514, 7-515
Bowling: Brown 27-2-107-3, Snow 20-3-68-0, D'Oliveira 15-2-62-0, Lock 32-3-129-1, Jones 29-1-108-2, Barrington 10-2-41-1

ENGLAND - First Innings

J H Edrich, c Lloyd b Carew	32
G Boycott, c Nurse b Rodriguez	62
M C Cowdrey, c Murray b Butcher	148
K F Barrington, lbw b Gibbs	48
T W Graveney, c Murray b Rodriguez	8
B L D'Oliveira, b Rodriguez	0
A P E Knott, not out	69
J A Snow, b Butcher	0
D J Brown, c Murray b Butcher	0
G A R Lock, lbw b Butcher	3
I J Jones, b Butcher	1
Extras (b14, lb10, w2, nb7)	33
Total	**414**

Fall of wickets: 1-86, 2-112, 3-245, 4-260, 5-260, 6-373, 7-377, 8-377, 9-381
Bowling: Sobers 36-8-87-0, Griffith 3-1-7-0, Gibbs 57-24-68-1, Rodriguez 35-4-145-3, Carew 25-18-23-1, Butcher 14-4-34-5, Lloyd 5-2-7-0, Nurse 2-2-0-0

WEST INDIES - Second Innings

S Camacho, c Graveney b Snow	31
M C Carew, not out	40
S M Nurse, run out	9
R B Kanhai, not out	2
Extras (b1, lb7, nb2)	10
Total (2 wkts dec)	**92**

Fall of wickets: 1-66, 2-88
Bowling: Brown 10-2-33-0, Snow 9-0-29-1, Jones 11-1-20-0

ENGLAND - Second Innings

J H Edrich, b Rodriguez	29
G Boycott, not out	80
M C Cowdrey, c Sobers b Gibbs	71
T W Graveney, b Gibbs	2
B L D'Oliveira, not out	12
Extras (b11, lb6, nb4)	21
Total (3 wkts)	**215**

Fall of wickets: 1-55, 2-173, 3-183,
Bowling: Sobers 14-0-47-0, Gibbs 16.4-1-76-2, Rodriguez 10-1-35-1, Carew 7-2-19-0, Butcher 5-1-17-0

England won by 7 wickets

A young Clive Lloyd has his stumps unceremoniously scattered by Jeff Jones

1974 Queen's Park Oval

FIFTH TEST, 30, 31 MARCH, 1-4 APRIL

Commentators: LANCE MURRAY, CHRISTOPHER MARTIN-JENKINS, RAFI KNOWLES

In a three-match series in England in 1973, the West Indies demonstrated the superiority with which they were to dominate for the rest of this decade and throughout the next. They won by two Tests to nil, a result which spelt the end of Ray Illingworth's time as England captain. The man chosen to lead the side in the Caribbean that winter was the Kent captain, Mike Denness.

In February the West Indies started the series where they had left off at Lord's in August. Keith Boyce, Bernard Julien and Gary Sobers dismissed the tourists for 131 in the first innings of the First Test at Port-of-Spain, which as usual was to host two matches in the series. In the West Indies innings Alvin

England captain Mike Denness hooks a ball from Inshan Ali to the boundary for four...but on 13 his innings was ended by the same bowler

Maybe one should, after all, take the rough with the smooth... Kallicharran and Greig manage to put the unsavoury events of the previous day behind them

Kallicharran made 158 and was at the centre of an unfortunate incident at the close of the second day when, as he left his crease to head for the pavilion after the last ball had been bowled, Tony Greig, fielding close in, threw his wicket down and the umpire had no choice but to give him out, run out. Pandemonium greeted the decision and after lengthy discussions in a beseiged pavilion the appeal was withdrawn by England.

Despite an opening partnership of 209 in the second innings, of which Geoff Boycott made 93 and Dennis Amiss — at the start of a year that was to bring him 1,379 runs — went on to make 174, England were beaten by seven wickets. After that start they collapsed to the spin of Gibbs and Sobers — food for thought for the return visit here. In the meantime, though, West Indies appeared to be on the point of taking a 2-0 lead in Jamaica. They were over two hundred ahead on first innings when Amiss staged a remarkable, almost single-handed, rescue act, making 262 not out and batting throughout a score of 432 for nine. In Barbados in the Third Test, Lawrence Rowe followed his Kingston century with a remarkable 302, which with a second century in the series from Kallicharran again gave West Indies a two hundred lead.

Test Match Special

Again, though, England clung on, this time with a defiant hundred from Keith Fletcher.

The Guyana Test, as is so often the case there, was eventually a victim of the weather, but not before England had seen some hopeful signs in the centuries from Amiss, again, and Tony Greig.

There was a noticeable turn around in Guyana, even though that Test match was so badly spoiled by rain. England made 448 and really it was the first time you got an inkling that England were coming into their own at that stage. I wrote at the time following that match that England flew to Trinidad for the final Test realising full well that there was everything to play for and almost nothing to lose.

TONY COZIER

Back in Port-of-Spain the expectations of what the pitch would do were expressed in the selection by each side of three men to spin the ball. England had Derek Underwood, Pat Pocock and Jack Birkenshaw, while the West Indies picked the local unorthodox slow left-armer, Inshan Ali, to join Gibbs and Sobers. On March 30th Denness won the toss and decided to bat, in a match that had been extended to six days because the series was undecided. During the series, despite making 93 in the First Test and 68 in the Second, Geoff Boycott had looked uncomfortable against new ball bouncers, to the extent that in Barbados he was dropped down the order.

Boycott must have been aghast when he was not sent in to open the innings in the Barbados Test. He went in at four, while Denness and Amiss opened the batting, and so he had something to prove in the final Test. And when Geoff Boycott has something to prove, he really can set his mind to it. The conditions were ideal for him, it was a slow pitch and he really put his head down and played as only Geoff Boycott can play.

TONY COZIER

Now he was back opening the innings and playing doggedly, which was as well for England, as the rest of the innings did not live up to the first wicket stand of 83. Early on, Boycott should have been run out, but the throw went wide. Amiss, his opening partner, made 44, but after that start wickets fell regularly. Denness made 13 and Fletcher 6, falling to Gibbs and Inshan Ali respectively. Greig made 19 of a stand of 32 for the fourth wicket before he was lbw to Gibbs, but Boycott, batting with Frank Hayes, was still there at the close.

He was out, though, within half an hour of the start of the second day, tantalisingly one short of his hundred as he nudged a ball from Julien down the leg-side for a diving catch by the wicket-keeper, Deryck Murray. That wicket precipitated something of a collapse as Hayes went for 24 to Ali and Alan Knott, making 33 not out watched the last five wickets go down for 55 in an hour and a quarter. England were all out for 267, with Gibbs and Inshan Ali having taken three wickets apiece.

It was a meagre total and made to look even more so by Roy Fredericks and Rowe who put on 110 for the first West Indian wicket. Pat Pocock broke the partnership, removing Fredericks for 67 and quickly adding the wicket of Kallicharran, caught and bowled for nought. At lunch on the third day, West Indies were only 59 runs behind with eight wickets in hand, but now, as Rowe reached his hundred the wickets started to tumble at the other end, as England introduced an unlikely off-spinner to their attack.

A*lthough England had three specialist spinners, Tony Greig was the one who did all the damage, which was the result of the advantage of his height and also the fact that he was bowling a little quicker on a slow pitch.*

TONY COZIER

A*pparently, Greig had bowled some off-spin during his school career in South Africa, but our first glimpse of his new style was when he experimented, with some success, in the Barbados Test. The West Indian batting line-up was packed with left-handers so his logic was easy to follow.*

CHRISTOPHER MARTIN-JENKINS

Tony Greig, in twenty balls, removed Clive Lloyd for 52, Sobers for nought, Kanhai for 2 and Murray for 2, and from 224 for two the West Indies had slumped to 232 for six, still 35 runs behind. Rowe was still there, moving steadily to another century, and he added 68 with the fast bowlers for the next two wickets, which took West Indies into the lead. Julien made 17 and Boyce 19, but both became victims of Greig. Rowe's innings of 123 then ended, caught off a Greig full toss. Greig finished with the wicket of Inshan Ali and the West Indies were all out for 305.

I*n one spell Greig took eight for 33 in 19.1 overs as an impromptu off-spinner. I doubt whether anyone in the game has ever come on to bowl away from his normal style and produced those sort of figures. It was the most remarkable spell of bowling of its sort that I have ever seen, because it exerted a complete psychological stranglehold over the West Indies.*

HENRY BLOFELD

Test Match Special

75

Geoff Boycott showed tremendous concentration during both innings in Trinidad after struggling in the previous two Tests

Greig's bowling had restricted West Indies' lead to 38 and kept England in a match they might very well have been batted out of by now. They had just retaken the lead early on the fourth morning when Amiss was bowled by one of Lloyd's gentle medium-paced deliveries for 16 and only five more runs came before Denness was run out.

Fletcher joined Boycott in an important partnership for the third wicket which, though it was interrupted by a few time-wasting showers, must have started to worry Kanhai and his team. In the final session of the day the new ball was taken, but the batsmen appeared to have weathered that particular storm, when Fletcher fell, bowled by Julien for 45 after a stand of 101. It was near enough to the close for Pocock to be sent in as night-watchman and when that fourth day ended England, at 157 for three, were 119 ahead with Boycott 81 not out.

On the fifth morning Boycott, appreciating the need for acceleration, was more aggressive. The night-watchman departed early and was quickly followed by Greig for 1 and Hayes for a duck, both of them to Julien. England were now 176 for six, only 138 ahead and no longer in a comfortable position. They did, though, now have the considerable fillip of seeing Boycott reach the hundred he had so narrowly missed in the first innings. He was 112 not out at lunch, which he and Knott took at 213 for six.

The first ball after the interval from Lance Gibbs, though, saw the demise of Boycott who was out without adding to his score.

His two innings were phenomenal performances. Boycott had tremendous concentration and a great love of batting which took him through. He still talks about that first innings 99. And when he got to 112 in the second innings, he was bowled by Lance Gibbs and the bail came off. Boycs stood there, implying that the ball had come off Deryck Murray's gloves, and when the umpires gave him out he went off like a snail — it was typical Boycott.

HENRY BLOFELD

Boycott had struggled in the previous Tests but his contribution here was immense. He booked in for bed and breakfast during both knocks and only a brilliant catch by Murray deprived him of a century in the first innings. His concentration was so intense in the second innings that he genuinely could not believe that Lance Gibbs had bowled him.

CHRISTOPHER MARTIN-JENKINS

After Boycott's departure the building up of some sort of target centred on Knott. With Geoff Arnold he added 32 for the ninth wicket and was last out to a controversial lbw decision for 44. It gave the greatest all-rounder of them all, Gary Sobers, the last wicket of his Test career in this, his last Test match. It also meant that England had been dismissed in mid-afternoon for 263 and that the West Indies had a day and a half to score a none-too-challenging 226, albeit on a worn pitch. A heavy rainstorm restricted their attempt on that target on the fifth day to forty minutes batting, during which time Rowe and Fredericks put on 30. So the issue for the final day was clear cut. Just 196 runs would be needed.

The first hour of the day was tense and one slip chance went down as 33 more runs were added. But in the first over after the mid-morning drinks break, Birkenshaw had Rowe lbw for 25. At the other end Denness had brought on his first innings hero, Greig, to bowl his own variety of off-breaks again and it accounted for the new batsman, Kallicharran, caught at slip second ball for his first Test 'pair'. And that

was not the end of this nightmare passage of play for West Indies, as Fredericks and Lloyd had a misunderstanding in mid-pitch over the wisdom of a second run and Boycott's throw ended the debate with Fredericks run out for 36. Three wickets had fallen in as many overs for the addition of two runs and suddenly the target, which had looked just round the corner at 63 for no wicket, was looking uncomfortably distant at 65 for three. Clive Lloyd restored the crowd's spirits with three well-struck boundaries off Birkenshaw, but at 84 his captain, Kanhai, chased a wide ball from Greig and was caught at slip. It left Greig with a few minutes before lunch to take his third wicket of the morning, a superbly athletic caught and bowled to remove Lloyd for 13. Again the pendulum had swung towards England. It was 85 for five.

Kallicharran gets a Test 'pair', caught by a jubillant Keith Fletcher (right) off the bowling of Greig with skipper Mike Denness (left) looking suitably delighted. England were now in a strong position to force home a win

Queen's Park Oval is one of the most beautiful grounds in the world, along with Newlands and the Adelaide Oval. It always has a carnival atmosphere, and the locals *were singing their calypsos when the West Indies were winning. But they became more muted when England got on top.*

HENRY BLOFELD

On the other side of the Atlantic, in Broadcasting House in London, plans were being hurriedly laid to bring a sort of Test Match Special onto the air late in the afternoon. Before that commentary was joined, though, Sobers and Murray were staging something of a rescue act. From that unpromising start, their sixth wicket partnership took West Indies past the hundred and then past the half-way point in their quest. The locals found their voices again. But at 135, Underwood deceived Sobers in the air and bowled the great man in his last Test innings for 20. Three more runs were added before Julien gave his Kent captain, Denness, a

West Indies captain Gary Sobers hooks imperiously for four, in a desperate attempt to stave off defeat

T e s t   M a t c h   S p e c i a l

straightforward catch at extra cover off the inevitable Greig. It was 138 for seven. The crowd were given another chance to believe in a West Indian victory, though, as Boyce started to add runs rapidly. But his eighth wicket partnership with Murray was ended by a familiar combination as Fletcher took his third slip catch of the innings off Greig to remove Murray for 33. At 166 for eight, West Indies needed another 60 to win.

The BBC did join the local commentary now, to witness a ninth wicket stand between Boyce and Inshan Ali which, surprisingly comfortably, reduced the target by 31. Denness took the gamble to give the new ball to Arnold, but he left Greig bowling his off-breaks at the other end.

RAFI KNOWLES *Another man now forward, and backward short-leg, and the two men on the off-side close in, and Greig bowls to Ali and Ali hits this and he might be out! Underwood is under it and he's caught. Hits it straight to Underwood. West Indies have lost their ninth wicket. Hitting the ball straight to Underwood, Inshan Ali, and then showing disgust at himself, walking in, hitting the bat on the ground and shaking the gloves off. So drawing even to a tenser finish. Inshan Ali, who put in a good partnership there with Boyce for 31. West Indies now needing 29 to win. It is veteran Lance Gibbs coming to the wicket.*

CHRISTOPHER MARTIN-JENKINS *Boyce is 34 not out. Gibbs is one not out and having taken the new ball, Denness will be persevering with Geoff Arnold who will be bowling from this northern end, the end from which we are looking out on this excited, animated scene with bright sunshine bathing the ground now. Here is Arnold right arm over the wicket, fast medium, running in again to bowl to Gibbs . . . and bowls him! And there it is, England have won. England have won the match and levelled the series. Lance Gibbs' leg stump knocked out of the ground. Denness, the England captain, takes two of the stumps and I have no doubt that he will want to keep one of them at least for the rest of his life. England have won this match by 27 runs. They have beaten the West Indies and levelled the series. The West Indies all out for a hundred and ninety-nine and a game which will never be forgotten by those who were here, especially on this unbearably tense final day, has ended and appropriately as the white helmeted policemen come to keep the crowds away from the players going back into the pavilion, the man who goes first up the pavilion steps is the tall fair-haired figure of Tony Greig.*

E
ngland played with real purpose and they had, of course, Boycott and Greig to thank for their victory. Greig's competitiveness and determination were the two factors that won that match for England on a pitch that was

ideally suited to Greig's off-spin — if you want to call it that. His height was a tremendous advantage and he bowled really well. A strong West Indies team were bowled out cheaply in both innings.

TONY COZIER

A West Indian batting line-up including Fredericks, Rowe, Kallicharran, Lloyd, Kanhai and Sobers, with Keith Boyce at number nine, should have comfortably scored the 226 runs required to win. After the game a disconsolate young West Indian asked me: 'How did we lose that game, man?' I couldn't answer him.

Greig's off-spin had a strange, temporary quality. He was vastly effective given the circumstances of the Test, but most critics assumed, correctly as it transpired, that he was unlikely to repeat the performance. It really was a one-off. He bowled at Underwood's pace and with his height could produce great deceptions of flight.

This was undoubtedly one of the most impressive Test match performances I have witnessed from an England team. Boycott and Greig made outstanding individual contributions but my abiding memory was how all eleven players produced a superlative fielding performance on the final afternoon.

CHRISTOPHER MARTIN-JENKINS

It was Greig's match in every way. One saw that he led by inspiration and was the likely successor to Denness as captain. It was an extraordinary performance because he psyched the West Indies out of a contest which they really should have won.

Greig always had this grip, but perhaps it went to his head and prompted the infamous 'grovel' remarks in 1976, which I'm sure he hasn't lived down, even to this day.

HENRY BLOFELD

It was a triumphant moment for the England captain, Mike Denness, though after his team's subsequent battering at the hands of Lillee and Thomson his tenure of office would last only another fifteen months. His successor would be the same blond hero who had started this Test series in blaze of controversy and ended it in a blaze of glory — Tony Greig. But he would not enjoy another Test victory over the West Indies. Indeed, not one of the next team of England cricketers to do so had yet started his Test career. Their moment of glory lay sixteen years ahead.

Test Match Special

Trinidadians indulge in rather premature celebrations after West Indies are left with the seemingly straight-forward task of making 226 runs in one-and-a half days

FINAL · SCORES

ENGLAND - First Innings

G Boycott, c Murray b Julien	99
D L Amiss, c Kanhai b Sobers	44
M H Denness, c Fredericks b Inshan	13
K W R Fletcher, c Kanhai b Gibbs	6
A W Greig, lbw b Gibbs	19
F C Hayes, c Rowe b Inshan	24
A P E Knott, not out	33
J Birkenshaw, c Lloyd b Julien	8
G G Arnold, run out	6
P I Pocock, c Lloyd b Inshan	0
D L Underwood, b Gibbs	4
Extras (b 2, lb 3, nb 6)	11
Total	**267**

Fall of wickets: 1-83, 2-114, 3-133, 4-165, 5-204, 6-212, 7-244, 8-257, 9-260
Bowling: Boyce 10-3-14-0, Julien 21-8-35-2, Sobers 31-16-44-1, Gibbs 34.3-11-70-3, Inshan 35-12-86-3, Lloyd 4-2-7-0

WEST INDIES - First Innings

R C Fredericks, c Fletcher b Pocock	67
L G Rowe, c Boycott b Greig	123
A I Kallicharran, c and b Pocock	0
C H Lloyd, c Knott b Greig	52
G S Sobers, c Birkenshaw b Greig	0
R B Kanhai, c and b Greig	2
D L Murray, c Pocock b Greig	2
B D Julien, c Birkenshaw b Greig	17
K D Boyce, c Pocock b Greig	19
Inshan Ali, lbw b Greig	5
L R Gibbs, not out	0
Extras (b 11, lb 4, nb 3)	18
Total	**305**

Fall of wickets: 1-110, 2-122, 3-224, 4-224, 5-226, 6-232, 7-270, 8-300, 9-300
Bowling: Arnold 8-0-27-0, Greig 36.1-10-86-8, Pocock 31-7-86-2, Underwood 34-12-57-0, Birkenshaw 8-1-31-0

ENGLAND - Second Innings

G Boycott, b Gibbs	112
D L Amiss, b Lloyd	16
M H Denness, run out	4
K W R Fletcher, b Julien	45
A W Greig, c Fredericks b Julien	1
F C Hayes, lbw b Julien	0
A P E Knott, lbw b Sobers	44
J Birkenshaw, c Gibbs b Inshan	7
G G Arnold, b Sobers	13
P I Pocock, c Kallicharran b Joyce	5
D Underwood, not out	1
Extras (lb 4, nb 11)	15
Total	**263**

Fall of wickets: 1-39, 2-44, 3-145, 4-169, 5-174, 6-176, 7-213, 8-226, 9-268
Bowling: Boyce 12-3-40-1, Julien 22-7-31-3, Sobers 24.2-9-36-2, Gibbs 50-15-85-1, Inshan 34-12-51-1, Lloyd 7-4-5-1

WEST INDIES - Second Innings

R C Fredericks, run out	36
L G Rowe, lbw b Birkenshaw	25
A I Kallicharran, c Fletcher b Greig	0
C H Lloyd, c and b Greig	13
G S Sobers, b Underwood	20
R B Kanhai, c Fletcher b Greig	7
D L Murray, c Fletcher b Greig	33
B D Julien, c Denness b Pocock	2
K D Boyce, not out	34
Inshan Ali, c Underwood b Greig	15
L R Gibbs, b Arnold	1
Extras (b 9, lb 2, nb 2)	13
Total	**199**

Fall of wickets: 1-63, 2-64, 3-65, 4-84, 5-85, 6-135, 7-138, 8-166, 9-197
Bowling: Arnold 5.3-1-13-1, Greig 33-8-70-5, Pocock 25-7-60-1, Underwood 15-7-19-1, Birkenshaw 10-1-24-1

England won by 27 runs

1976 The Oval

FIFTH TEST, 12-14, 16, 17 AUGUST

Commentators: JOHN ARLOTT, BRIAN JOHNSTON, DON MOSEY, TONY COZIER
Summarisers: TREVOR BAILEY, FRED TRUEMAN

*I like to think that people are building these West Indians up,
because I'm not really sure that they're as good as everyone thinks
they are. Sure they've got a couple of fast bowlers, but really I don't
think we're going to run into anything any more sensational than
Thomson and Lillee and so really I'm not worried about them.
You must remember the West Indians — these guys — if they get on
top they're magnificent cricketers. But if they're down, they grovel.
And I intend, with the help of Closey and a few others,
to make them grovel.*
TONY GREIG speaking on BBC TV before the series.

Tony Greig's infamous remarks, expressing his aim to make the West
Indies 'grovel', were to haunt him through that summer, after they had
been made in a BBC television interview previewing the forthcoming
Test series. They certainly concentrated the West Indies minds.

*I think you've got to understand the whole political
situation vis-a-vis South Africa and South Africans in the
West Indian consciousness. To have a white South African
— albeit captaining England — using a word like 'grovel'
certainly raised the hackles of the West Indies team and
committed them even more fiercely to winning that series.*
TONY COZIER

The year 1976 was a West Indian summer in England in its endless
sunshine and in its cricket as Clive Lloyd, who had taken over the
captaincy since England had last played his side, unveiled his new-look
side. With no England tour the previous winter, the events of the West
Indies tour of Australia had been followed by the British public with
more attention than usual. The ease of Australia's 5-1 Test victory was
surprising, not least to the West Indians themselves, and it probably
helped to inspire Greig to make his challenging remarks. But there was a
glimpse of the shape of things to come in their one victory on the
lightning-fast pitch in Perth where Michael Holding, in his second Test
match took four first innings wickets and Andy Roberts took seven in the
second innings and nine in the match to ensure that big hundreds by

Test Match Special

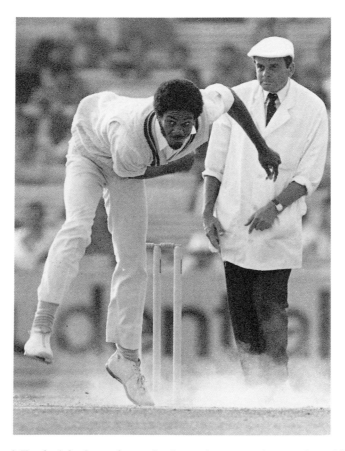

Fourteen wickets for Michael Holding at the Oval...and it's Tony Greig who has to do the grovelling

Lloyd and Fredericks brought an innings victory to the touring side.

Holding was a totally new name in England and, although he had not made a tremendous impact on the series in terms of wickets, he was reported to be really fast. Roberts had had three seasons with Hampshire, so, although he had only come into the Test side during England's last Caribbean tour, his class and speed were known. During the previous winter two batsmen already known in English county cricket had played their first Test for the West Indies in India. They, too, were to have quite an impact on the series in England — Viv Richards and Gordon Greenidge. Richards did so immediately, in the First Test at Trent Bridge, where he made 232, but a first Test century for David Steele was at the heart of the England resistance that eventually earned a draw. Roberts took ten wickets at Lord's, but the bowling of Snow and Underwood more than evened up the contest which ended in another, rather closer, draw, after the third day had — unusually for that summer — been lost to rain. Old Trafford was a remarkable Test match, in which Gordon Greenidge's first innings century rescued his side from 26 for four and his second innings one rammed home the advantage given to them by Holding's five for 17. For good measure, Richards also scored another hundred and two old England stalwarts, Brian Close and John

Edrich, experienced the full hostility of a short-pitched barrage in their last Test. The West Indies won by a massive 425 runs. They won, too, in a classically thrilling Test at Leeds, where rapid centuries by the West Indian openers, Fredericks and Greenidge, were answered by rearguard ones from Greig and Knott. The effectiveness, though, of a four-pronged fast attack — the new plan — was shown in the sharing of the wickets between Roberts, Holding, the young Wayne Daniel and the veteran Vanburn Holder.

So the series was already won 2-0 when the teams came to the Oval for the Fifth and final Test in the middle of that hot August, when all cricket grounds were parched and the open spaces of Kennington looked like an unforgiving desert. The Oval pitch of those days was regarded by bowlers as a featherbed; a batsman's paradise, so when Lloyd won the toss he had no hesitation in batting. There was one early setback, though.

JOHN ARLOTT *A typical Test opening, a little bit of sparring, the bowlers doing a little bit with the new ball, the batsmen not really bothered about forcing the pace at the moment, waiting for the shine to go off and the bowlers' freshness to subside a little and a chance to say for those who have only just tuned in, John Snow, because of a muscle injury, is out of the England 12. Now Willis bowls to Greenidge, covers up, raps him on the pad and he's out. Out lbw covering up. Squaring right up and Willis brought it back from outside the off-stump. Umpire Alley gave it due consideration, Greenidge out and I've no doubt kicking himself. Lbw Willis, nought. West Indies 5 for one.*

FRED TRUEMAN *It was a pretty good delivery that. It pitched I should think off-stump or just outside and came back in off the seam. It kept a bit low and I think it took Greenidge a bit more by surprise than anything and he looked bang in front from where I'm sitting and umpire Bill Alley had no hesitation in upholding the appeal, and I feel that Bob Willis will be very, very pleased with that because the West Indies batsmen really looked as though they'd got all the time in the world and I feel sure that Greenidge will be very upset with himself missing out on this type of wicket .*

Greenidge out for nought, but swaggering to the wicket was the supremely confident figure of Viv Richards. It was to be some time before England achieved another breakthrough. Greig decided not to be drawn by the evidence of an early wicket for Willis and had Underwood in the attack very quickly, but the second wicket pair had added 154 before the off-spinner, Geoff Miller, playing in his first Test, had Fredericks well caught at cover for 71. Derek Underwood had to wait to the last half hour of the day for his first wicket after another large stand, this time of 191 for the third wicket. Lawrence Rowe was stumped for

70, to give Alan Knott the dismissal that took him past Godfrey Evans' Test record of 219.

During that long partnership Richards had dominated and had gone to his seventh Test hundred of the calendar year and his third of that series. He was on the verge of another double hundred when Rowe's wicket fell.

Kent and England wicket-keeper Alan Knott takes a sharp stumping chance to dismiss Lawrence Rowe off Derek Underwood's bowling, of which he had a canny understanding

TREVOR BAILEY *Seeing Fred come into the box Brian, a little thing occurred to me. I wonder how many times Fred played in a Test match when the score was over 350 on the first day and he'd only bowled nine overs?*

BRIAN JOHNSTON *Yes, it'd be interesting. Anyhow at the moment we're going to see if Richards can get his 200. He's one nine nine. The bowler is going to be Greig bowling from the Vauxhall end. Three men on the off-side. and in he comes now. Will this be it? The field coming in to save the single and he clips this one away and that is it. It goes down to square-leg. He's made 200 and I'm afraid there's an invasion of the pitch from all round. This is a pity because they've been very good up till now. Unfortunately they're all coming on the pitch. This is a tremendous pity. They were asked not to and poor Richards is being mobbed. This is very, very sad. This not only delays everything it spoils Richards' concentration and people's enjoyment of this marvellous innings. He's made 200 and Bill give us the facts so we can forget the people because they're going to be about 3 minutes clearing the ground.*

BILL FRINDALL *It's taken him 5 hours and 37 minutes. That's 337 minutes. He's faced 263 balls and he has hit 24 fours. It's his second double century of the series.*

In the previous Test, Richards had passed Bobby Simpson's record number of runs for a calendar year of 1,381. The next day he was to take his total for the year to 1,710 and his total for the series to 829.

It was a tremendous performance by Richards. Every time he came to the wicket one expected him to get big runs. It had all changed for him in Australia when he'd been making thirties and forties and then getting out when he was looking good. It was felt that he should be used to open the batting and really put up against it right away. He opened in the last two Tests, scored a century in Adelaide and 50 and 98 in Melbourne and that really seemed to have changed his entire attitude to batting. It seemed to have given him an appetite for runs.

TONY COZIER

Test Match Special

Richards hammers a four through the covers...and pours on the misery for the England bowlers on his way to a monumental score of 291

Richards was now in partnership with his captain, Clive Lloyd, and on the second day the runs came even more freely. The milestones flashed by. Four hundred came up, Lloyd reached a half-century, Richards 250, five hundred was passed and now thoughts turned to another great innings at the Oval, Len Hutton's 364 and Gary Sobers' world record Test score one run further on.

TREVOR BAILEY *And though Brian and myself may be getting a little bit weary of this massacre in the sun, it's a wonderful afternoon for Bill Frindall who is having an absolute ball because statistics are going left,*

Test Match Special

right and centre. It's a great afternoon for statisticians.

BRIAN JOHNSTON *You can hear the sparks coming out of his ears with the excitement. Because if Richards does pass Hutton's and then Sobers' record, it is going to be absolutely electric in here. Anyhow, he's a long way off at the moment. He's two eighty-seven, Richards. He's waiting to face Greig coming in now, bowls this one well pitched up. And he drives that one. And that one's gone up to the boundary, up on the Vauxhall end and that's four runs as it goes bouncing up there against the white stand and people up here at the far end stand up and cheer. And that one hit over the top there and Richards may be going for the six he hasn't got but he's at the moment 291. 524 for three. Selvey's right out by the Vauxhall stand; the little covered bit of stand up there at long-on and here's Greig coming in again. And this one's outside the leg-stump and this one's clipped away. It isn't. He goes to clip it away but doesn't and trickles down the pitch off the pad and is fielded by Greig. He goes for a big sweep down to Woolmer who is down at backward square-leg by the scoreboard where most of the noise comes from but it's nice and peaceful, touch wood, at the moment, isn't it? Here's Greig coming up again to bowl to Richards. Bowls this one. Well pitched up outside the off-stump and there he's bowled! Richards is out. There's no question of a record. Greig has got his wicket and he's out for 291 and I think we must just let the applause from the crowd register as he walks back to the pavilion. He's taken his cap off. Just listen. Everyone standing up all round the ground, in the pavilion, paying homage to this really great innings and King comes in. Collis King comes in as the people gradually sit down again. Well your pithy comments on that knock, Trevor.*

TREVOR BAILEY *Well, we've already almost run out of superlatives. At the end I think undoubtedly he was getting a little tired. He went for an off-drive and was bowled through the gate by a very reasonable off-break. He was trying to hit it through the off-side. He'd been down the wicket and hit Greig over the top. A good off-break bowled through the gate trying to hit it against the spin through the covers. A tired end to a superb innings. It is the best innings we've seen in this series.*

The departure of Richards for 291 was by no means the end of the massacre. Rather it was the start of the real slog. Lloyd went on to make 84, Collis King a very rapid 63, Deryck Murray 36 and Michael Holding gave it the long handle as the West Indies passed their highest ever total against England. Greig had used nine bowlers when Underwood finally bowled Holding and Lloyd declared at 687 for eight. It left England twelve overs to face on the second evening and, despite their gruelling time roasting in the field for two days they more than survived what might have been an awkward session, making 34 runs. This was England's fifth different opening partnership of the series, consisting of Bob Woolmer — who had been moved up the order following the honourable discharge given to Edrich and Close after the Old Trafford Test — and Dennis Amiss, who had been hit on the head by Holding while batting for the MCC in an early season encounter and had only now returned to the Test side with a very much more square-on stance. The West Indies had stuck to their four-pronged pace attack even for the lifeless Oval pitch, with no specialist spinner in the side. Expert opinion said it would cost them the chance of winning the match, even with such a huge first innings score. But their breakthrough was not long in coming on the third morning.

JOHN ARLOTT *About six feet tall with quite a good pair of shoulders, but a lithe man rather than a heavyweight, Holding comes up like the sprinter he once was, high on his toes, lovely smooth approach. A scrub of the ball now, turns, changes the ball over from left hand to right and at full tilt bowls to Woolmer and appeals for lbw and he's out, moving across the stumps, and umpire Bird waited just a moment, checked all things and gave Woolmer out. Indeed he was out lbw Holding, beaten by pace. Lbw Holding eight and England are 47 for one.*

TREVOR BAILEY *I'm glad I didn't say it but until that moment Woolmer had looked extremely safe and sound. I think he was simply deceived by the sheer pace of the ball. On the back foot, in line, probably came back a fraction. Done by pace. Played very well until that one delivery.*

Joining Amiss after Woolmer's departure for 8 was David Steele, who had been hauled out of county cricket the previous year at a comparatively late stage of his career to do the job of combatting Lillee and Thomson, a job he had fulfilled admirably. He had started this series with a century and now he and Amiss started to build a partnership that suggested that England were not overawed by the enormity of their task.

JOHN ARLOTT *It's Holding then to Amiss. Amiss takes guard, with his backlift towards third man. Holding bowls to him. He moves into line. Plays it out on the on-side. There's a quick attempt there by Daniel to run out Steele. A very fast piece of work. He was safely home and these two have now put on a hundred.*

A hundred in 109 minutes. That's not such slow going as one might have expected or even feared. And the West Indian field now split up, two slips and a gully, well three slips really, and then five saving the one, and one out. And this for Holding. Comes in now, bowls to Steele and Steele goes forward and is hit on the pad. And he's out. lbw. Looks with some doubt at umpire Alley. A slight, sad wag of the head. Steele lbw for 44.

That hundred partnership and Steele's demise for 44 was followed by the very brief appearance of Chris Balderstone, playing the second and last Test of his career. He was yorked by the sheer pace of Holding for a duck and England were 151 for three. Peter Willey was the new batsman, a gritty performer for sure, and just the person to see Dennis Amiss to three figures.

*T*his match was the origin of 'The bowler's Holding, the batsman's Willey,' which I can't remember saying, but someone wrote to me to say that I should be more careful about the younger listeners.

BRIAN JOHNSTON

TONY COZIER *Michael Holding turns with all three wickets to his credit. One sixty-four for three England and Dennis Amiss within four runs of a century — 96. Amiss drives. This could be it. The ball racing away, that will be it, Amiss' hundred. On his return to Test cricket for England Dennis Amiss reaches a hundred. England one sixty-eight for three. The first to congratulate him was a chap who came from the West Indian section. There are a few youngsters and now a real character who has the West Indian players convulsing in laughter and who looks as if he is going to kiss Amiss. One sixty-eight for three. Bearded, dishevelled, everything out including his jacket and his shirt out of his trousers and Dennis Amiss who has collected I think a quid or two from supporters who have come on to the ground has now handed it over to umpire Bird at square-leg and I'm sure really pleased, Dennis Amiss, at this century on his return to Test cricket. A fine innings indeed made out of 168 for three and gained with a superb off-drive off Holding for four.*

TREVOR BAILEY *There is a word called pedigree and some batsmen have it and some batsmen haven't and Dennis Amiss, despite his long list of failures, has pedigree and by pedigree I mean the fact that in first class cricket they average at least forty and in Test cricket they average around forty. They've got class and he's got class. But there's never been any doubt about that and a hundred out of 168 just sort of shows it.*

The Amiss-Willey partnership continued to prosper, adding 128 before Collis King, the fifth seamer in the attack, had Willey caught for 33. As Greig joined Amiss, though, at 279 for 4 there was still good cause to believe that England might reach the 488 they needed to avoid the follow-on.

TREVOR BAILEY *Three hundred up and one feels that England must have a splendid chance of saving this match, something I've felt right from the very start, at least from 6:20 yesterday evening.*

TONY COZIER *So it's Holding who will continue. We have bright sunshine. We haven't had sunshine all day, which has been rather rare in this summer of sunshine, but right now the sun streaming across the ground, shadows of the players long as Lloyd, perhaps the longest of the lot, comes*

T e s t   M a t c h   S p e c i a l

Amiss cuts to the boundary on his way to a double century, but England were still over 250 runs adrift on first innings' totals

back to his position at fourth slip having given instructions to Holding. Holding now starting to Greig. Greig is 12. 303 for four. Holding's first ball to Greig. He's bowled him! Greig is bowled, right through him, hitting across the yorker and Greig is bowled. A partial invasion of the ground by some West Indian supporters as Greig is bowled by Holding for 12. England are 303 for five and they're coming on to the ground, West Indian supporters, more and more now. They're coming across the pitch as well. Umpire Bird is trying to keep them off the ground, off the pitch. Some of the West Indian players beseeching them not to walk across the pitch. Lloyd is there, so is King, so is Daniel. Amiss is also asking them to keep off. It seems as if, well, it's fruitless really. All across the ground they're mobbing Holding now. They're lifting him up. They're still walking on the pitch. . .umpire Bird has gone down on his hands and knees.

After the 'grovel' remark, the greatest moment for Michael Holding was when he uprooted two of Tony Greig's stumps. I remember him pumping the air with his arm. It was the one wicket they really wanted.

FRED TRUEMAN

Test Match Special

England physio Laurie Brown attends rather vigorously to a pain-stricken Graham Gooch after the England captain has his hand broken by Ezra Moseley during the second innings of the 1990 Trinidad Test *(Photo Adrian Murrell/Allsport)*

Test Match Special

Gordon Greenidge
makes hay at the Oval
in 1988. West Indies
cruised to an eight-
wicket victory and so
wrapped up a rather
one-sided series 3-0
*(Photo Adrian
Murrell/Allsport)*

The scenic setting of Sabina Park, Kingston (*above, photo Adrian Murrell/Allsport*). The 1989-90 touring side rewrote the record books with a remarkable win here in the first Test. By the time the sides came together in Antigua, however, the script had taken on a more familiar look as England batsman Robin Smith (*opposite, photo Ben Radford/Allsport*) would testify

Test Match Special

Test Match Special

Test Match Special

Graham Gooch and Allan Lamb looking forlorn as rain intervenes during the 1990 Jamaica Test match. However, the gods were smiling on England and the next day dawned bright and sunny, enabling the tourists to clinch an historic victory
(Photo Graham Morris)

The prized scalp of Viv Richards falls to Devon Malcolm, and West Indies are in big trouble at Sabina Park in 1990 *(Photo Adrian Murrell/Allsport)*

The crowd invasion that greeted Greig's wicket was serious enough for the umpires to take the players off the field and nine minutes were lost, which helped the night-watchman, Underwood, to stay to the close of that third day, with England 304 for 5. Amiss was 178 not out. Another nineteen runs were added on the Monday morning before Holding bowled Underwood for 4. His Kent colleague, Alan Knott, came in to join Amiss, now nearing a double century.

JOHN ARLOTT *Gives the bat another little twirl and settles this very open looking stance, showing all three stumps to the bowler until now when he covers up, completely with both legs and plays that off his legs for four runs. Four runs just backward of square. Takes him to 199 and England to three thirty-two for six, and how paltry the English innings would have looked without this score of Amiss'. Three three-two for six but only one three three by his seven colleagues.*
BILL FRINDALL *Of which 31 are extras.*
JOHN ARLOTT *Well this means that he has scored almost two-thirds of the runs from the bat. 301 from the bat of which he's scored 199. And Holding bowls to him and Amiss plays that past Greenidge again for four runs and now he's actually scored two-thirds of England's runs from the bat — 203 out of 336 for six. And cheerful applause from the West Indians still applauding him, Fredricks, Julien, Lloyd, Greenidge, Murray. I suppose that ought to convince anybody that he has conquered this problem.*

I thought that Amiss played a great innings, after being hit on the head in the MCC match at Lord's by some of the fastest bowling I have ever seen. It was remarkable to go out and do what he did in his first Test back.

BRIAN JOHNSTON

Amiss had come back into the England side with a most peculiar change in his technique as he would come right across the stumps and leave his leg-stump exposed. It seemed inevitable that he would have to get bowled around his legs. It was a great change from the man we had seen get that wonderful double hundred in Jamaica to save the match in 1974. In the end here his leg-stump was hit, though he had made over two hundred runs at that stage.

FRED TRUEMAN

TONY COZIER *It's the smallest crowd we've had for the Test match so far but I say that one must also remember that the crowds on the first three*

Overjoyed at claiming another victim. Michael Holding bowled beautifully in both innings, generating alarming pace on a slow wicket *days were, on the first two at least, were packed. The great gates were closed. I'm not too sure if they were on Saturday but it also was a very big crowd on Saturday and the crowd today, even though it is the smallest of the match, is still a very good one. Here's Holding now. In to Amiss and bowls him behind his back, leg-stump. Amiss bowled Holding, coming too far across as he had always threatened to do, shuffling across his stumps, the leg-stump hit. Holding's sixth wicket and a magnificent innings from Amiss ended, bowled Holding 203, England three forty-two for seven.*

The wicket of Amiss was Holding's sixth. He had to wait for his seventh until an eighth wicket stand of 69 between Knott and Miller had taken England past 400 and Knott to 50. But in two balls Holding bowled Knott and the new batsman Mike Selvey. He missed the hat-trick and 24 more runs were added before Miller's first Test innings of 36 was ended by Holder and England were all out for 435. Holding had taken an amazing eight for 92.

It was a tremendous piece of bowling, especially because of the conditions. More recently in hindsight he has said that if he had had to bowl on that pitch later in his career when he was more experienced that he would have taken one look at it — as the other fast bowlers did and said, 'Look, this is a flat, slow pitch,' and not extended himself. But he reckons that because he was young and inexperienced and full of enthusiasm, he never let that put him off. He just ran up and bowled as fast as he possibly could and it emphasised that once you are bowling fast and straight it really doesn't matter whether the pitch is fast or slow or a pudding.

TONY COZIER

Lloyd decided to let Holding have a rest before unleashing him on England again, so he declined to enforce the follow-on. Fredericks and Greenidge went in again in mid-afternoon to make merry in adding to the lead of 252. And they really did enjoy themselves as England tried desperately to defend the wide-open parched spaces of the Oval. In 140 minutes batting they increased the lead by a significant 182 runs without being separated.

TONY COZIER *Willis back to his mark. Phenomenal field to look at when you divert your attention from the middle of the pitch and look to the fielders all over the place. Greenidge goes to deflect this ball down to fine-leg, gets too far across, misses the shot. The end of the over. Declaration. The declaration has come then with the West Indies 182 for no wicket, 85 to Greenidge, 86 to Fredricks. The West Indies have declared. The West*

Indies have declared and Tony Greig has gone on his hands and knees and for the West Indies spectators and to the delight of the West Indies spectators now smiling all over his face, gone on his hands and knees and for three or four paces has, in his own words, 'grovelled' in front of the West Indian spectators. Well, that was a good little touch by Tony Greig and I think the West Indian spectators appreciated it. One eighty-two for no wicket at the end of the West Indies innings, 85 to Greenidge and 86 to Fredricks.

The West Indies with that declaration left themselves twenty minutes on the fourth evening and the whole of the last day to bowl England out. Lloyd, who had seen the Indians score 406 to beat his side earlier that year had left his opponents this time an impossible 435 to win. English hopes were reasonably high, though, that they could survive for a draw. Amiss and Woolmer started the innings that evening as if they were indeed going to get the runs. The twenty minutes yielded 43 runs. But the next morning was a different story as the West Indies hero of the first innings got to work again.

JOHN ARLOTT *Holding, bowling remarkably enough on this warm morning in a sweater, turns away at the Vauxhall end. Moves lightly up, well up on his toes. Bowls to Amiss and Amiss plays this off his hip down to long-leg where Roberts comes racing round, picks up and returns. Two runs. Perfect return to Murray there beside the stumps. And Amiss giving no real sign of trouble with what must be appreciable bruising on his arm. He steps back from the stumps for a moment then gives that habitual twirl of his bat and steps into his guard as Holding comes sprinting in. Bowls to him outside the off-stump and he's caught. He's caught by Greenidge, a very tentative stroke outside the off-stump and he edged it straight to second slip. The simplest possible slip catch. Greenidge held it and England are 49 for one. Amiss caught Greenidge, bowled Holding 16. Holding's ninth wicket of the match.*

Holding continued to bowl menacingly, and it wasn't long before he struck again.

JOHN ARLOTT *Holding comes in, bowls to Woolmer and Woolmer drives that crisply through the on-side field, wide of wide mid-on for four. A crisp clean stroke which takes him to 30 and the total to 54. It's his sixth four. Holding again then comes in, bowls to Woolmer and Woolmer gropes for that and there's an appeal for a catch at the wicket and he's out. . . and umpire Bird deliberated some time there before he gave him out but it was a stroke rather like Amiss', the ball was a little higher, the deflection was finer. It went to the wicket-keeper and Woolmer is out then, caught Murray, bowled Holding. Holding's second wicket of the innings, his tenth of the match and he made 30.*

BRIAN JOHNSTON *Holding runs up now, past Dickie Bird and bowls this one and that's yorked him. Off-stump knocked clean out of the ground. It was probably a full pitch on the stump there and poor old Balderstone has made two noughts. Bowled Holding both times. Beaten undoubtedly for pace once again and England are for 64 for three and in the sort of trouble that many of their supporters hoped there wouldn't be today.*

Thirteen runs later and England's misery was further compounded, as the England captain prepared to face the bowling.

BRIAN JOHNSTON *Holding comes in, to Greig, bowls there, and he's bowled him! His leg-stump knocked right back plus the middle stump.*

BILL FRINDALL *He is the first West Indies bowler to take 12 wickets in a Test match against England and only one other bowler, Roberts, has done so in any Test match for the West Indies.*

FRED TRUEMAN *What a magnificent delivery by Holding. He knows this high backlift of Greig's which they've played on, and he came up the first delivery and bowled the perfect yorker on the leg-stump and knocked the leg-stump right out of the ground leaving Tony Greig completely nonplussed.*

The first hour of the last day had sealed England's fate. Four more wickets for Holding and one for the deserving Holder had wiped away the top half of the batting order, with the exception of David Steele, while only 35 runs were added. Steele went on to make 42. It was to be his last Test innings, as the selectors reckoned that he had served his purpose against the Australian and West Indian pace and did not pick him for India that winter. With Knott, who made his second half-century of the match, he added 70 runs for the sixth wicket. Holding was rested while Holder and Richards removed two more batsmen and then he returned to bowl Knott in the first over of a new spell for 57. Roberts dismissed Underwood, but it was only fitting that Holding should deliver the coup de grace.

JOHN ARLOTT *203 for nine. Four to Selvey and Willis has not scored and we have had a dramatic change in fortunes of the match with three wickets falling very quickly. It was 196 for six in fact at one stage and then Miller was bowled by Richards for 24, Knott was bowled by Holding for 57 and Underwood was caught by Lloyd off Roberts for two. It's now 203 for nine. All the West Indian supporters just waiting for this last wicket to fall. To rush on to the field. I'm sure that when it does fall all the players will be trying to beat them to the dressing rooms. In comes Holding. On the way now and hits him on the pad and he's out leg-before-wicket. The West Indies have won. Willis out leg-before-wicket to Holding. Holding's sixth*

wicket in the innings, his fourteenth in the match. Souvenirs have been grabbed. Here come the West Indian supporters swarming over the ground. Selvey is being jostled out in the middle so are other players and the umpires. Jubilation for the West Indian supporters and the West Indies have won. Selvey wants to get away in fact. Someone is trying to take his bat away from him. He is being jostled by spectators. They are looking for souvenirs. He has got a stump himself and his bat and his cap and some of the spectators wanting to get some souvenirs off him, trying to snatch them from his hand and he has to be protected by some policemen as he comes back. The West Indies have won this final Test match then. England all out for 203. The West Indies have won by 231 runs. Willis leg-before-wicket, bowled by Holding without scoring. Holding's sixth wicket in the innings. All the West Indian spectators in front jubilant, and calling for their heroes. The West Indies have won by 231 runs. They've won the series 3-0. England all out for 203. A victory which has been achieved primarily because of the batting of Richards in the first innings supported by Fredricks and Rowe and in this, in the England innings, first and second, through the bowling of Michael Holding.

Amazing scenes at the Oval as West Indies fans await the appearance of their team on the members' balcony after the match

Test   Match   Special

FINAL · SCORES

WEST INDIES - First Innings

R C Fredericks, c Balderstone b Miller		71
C G Greenidge, lbw b Willis		0
I V A Richards, b Greig		291
L G Rowe, st Knott b Underwood		70
C H Loyd, c Knott b Greig		84
C L King, c Selvey b Balderstone		63
D L Murray, c and b Underwood		36
V A Holder, not out		13
M A Holding, b Underwood		32
Extras (b1, lb17, nb9)		27
Total		687

Fall of wickets: 1-5, 2-159, 3-350, 4-524, 5-547, 6-640, 7-642, 8-687

Bowling: Willis 15-3-73-1, Selvey 15-0-67-0, Underwood 60-15-165-3, Woolmer 9-0-44-0, Miller 27-4-106-1, Balderstone 16-0-80-1, Greig 34-5-96-2, Willey 3-0-11-0, Steele 3-0-18-0

ENGLAND - First Innings

D L Amiss, b Holding		203
R A Woolmer, lbw b Holding		8
D S Steele, lbw b Holding		44
J C Balderstone, b Holding		0
P Willey, c Fredericks b King		33
A W Greig, b Holding		12
D L Underwood, b Holding		4
A P E Knott, b Holding		50
G Miller, c sub b Holder		36
M W W Selvey, b Holding		0
R G D Willis, not out		5
Extras (b8, lb11, nb21)		40
Total		435

Fall of wickets: 1-47, 2-147, 3-151, 4-279, 5-303, 6-323, 7-342, 8-411, 9-411

Bowling: Roberts 27-4-102-0, Holding 33-9-92-8, Holder 27.5-7-75-1, Daniel 10-1-30-0, Fredericks 11-2-36-0, Richards 14-4-30-0, King 7-3-30-1

WEST INDIES - Second Innings

R C Fredericks, not out		86
C G Greenidge, not out		85
Extras (b4, lb1, w1, nb5)		11
Total (0 wkt)		182

Bowling: Willis 7-0-48-0, Selvey 9-1-44-0, Underwood 9-2-38-0, Woolmer 5-0-30-0, Greig 2-0-11-0

ENGLAND - Second Innings

D L Amiss, c Greenidge b Holding		16
R A Woolmer, c Murray b Holding		30
D S Steele, c Murray b Holding		42
J C Balderstone, b Holding		0
P Willey, c Greenidge b Holder		1
A W Greig, b Holding		1
D L Underwood, c Lloyd b Roberts		2
A P E Knott, b Holding		57
G Miller, b Richards		24
M W W Selvey, not out		4
R G D Willis, lbw b Holding		0
Extras (b15, lb3 w8)		26
Total		203

Fall of wickets: 1-49, 2-54, 3-64, 4-77, 5-78 6-148, 7-196, 8-196, 9-202

Bowling: Roberts 13-4-37-1, Holding 20.4-6-57-6, Holder 14-5-29-2, Fredericks 12-5-33-0, Richards 11-6-11-1, King 6-2-9-0, Lloyd 2-1-1-0

West Indies won by 231 runs

England captain Tony Greig was a victim of Holding's sheer pace in both innings

1981 Kensington Oval and Sabina Park

THIRD TEST, 13-15, 17, 18 MARCH
FIFTH TEST, 10-12, 14, 15 APRIL

Commentators: DON MOSEY, TONY COZIER, REDS PEREIRA, EVERTON WEEKES

Ian Botham and Ken Barrington in happier times before the ill-fated 1980-81 tour to the Caribbean

In 1980 Mike Brearley, of his own volition, ended his successful tenure of the England captaincy (though he had never captained against the West Indies in a Test match). His influence at that stage was such that his recommendation for his successor was taken up by the selectors and Ian Botham, at the age of twenty-four, was appointed captain for the home series against the West Indies. It was won 1-0 by the visitors, after the weather took a powerful hand in four of the Tests. Although his previously devastating form seemed to have deserted him during the summer, Botham was reappointed to lead the side in the Caribbean that coming winter.

> Mike Brearley thought Botham was the right choice, which was the one decision of Brearley's that I always found most extraordinary from such a brilliant thinker about the game. I suppose, all things considered, Botham did what he could. But I don't think the intricacies of the game ever held his attention long enough for him to examine the ways to help players as a captain.
>
> HENRY BLOFELD

Test Match Special

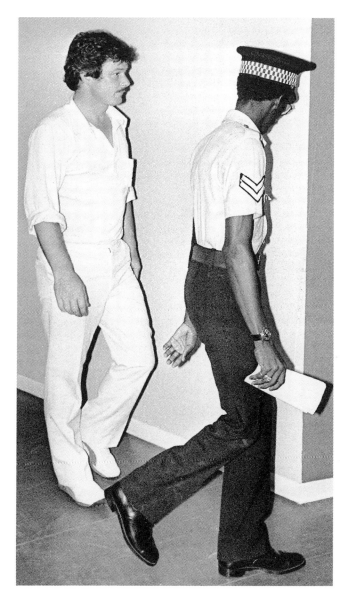

Robin Jackman's previous links with South Africa created an uproar in Guyana, as a result of which he was served with a deportation order. The second Test was abandoned and for a time the future of the whole tour was in doubt

It was to be a troubled tour and the first problem arose in the second match, when the vice-captain, Bob Willis, injured his knee. Without him there, West Indies won the First Test in Trinidad by an innings and the day after that match Willis was flown home to be replaced, in time for the second Test in Guyana, by Robin Jackman.

Jackman had spent several English winters in South Africa, playing for Western Province and then Rhodesia in the Currie Cup, though this did not immediately seem a problem when he arrived in the middle of the night in Georgetown. Indeed he was by no means the only member of the side with playing connections with South Africa. However, soon after his arrival in Guyana, a journalist at the other end of the Caribbean wrote an article attacking his presence on the tour. The Guyana government investigated and, just as the team returned from a one-day international up-country, Jackman was served with a deportation order. Inevitably the Test and County Cricket Board's response was that if Jackman had to go, then the whole team would leave with him. The Second Test was abandoned and for the next two tours, England did not go to Guyana. Their bolt-hole was Barbados, a week earlier than had originally been planned, where the team waited anxiously in their hotel while the future of the tour was decided.

It was a very difficult situation for Robin Jackman, who was being used as a pawn by the Marxist government in Guyana. Many people would have crumbled, but Robin is a splendid chap who carried it off awfully well.

HENRY BLOFELD

It took a meeting of the foreign ministers of the countries to which England still had to go. Eventually it was decided that the tour would go ahead, but there were four or five days when there was considerable doubt.

TONY COZIER

After nearly a week of uncertainty, the beautiful island of Barbados suddenly became a most welcoming place to be. An extra one-day game against the island was laid on — which England won — and then, exactly a month after the start of the First Test the next one — the Third — got under way. On 13th March, Ian Botham won the toss and, encouraged by a look of greenness in the pitch, put the West Indies in. Dilley and Botham with the new ball could not make an initial breakthrough, so Botham brought on Robin Jackman for his first bowl in Test cricket.

DON MOSEY *Jackman, feeling the heat already, mops his brow, as he turns and starts to move away from us. Bowls to Greenidge, who is forward and he's out! Caught at first slip by Gooch, and in his first over in Test cricket, Robin Jackman strikes the first blow for England. Greenidge, caught Gooch, bowled Jackman, for 14 and West Indies are 24 for one.*

A wicket for Jackman with his fifth ball in Test cricket, and almost immediately it looked even better for England as Dilley got the most prized scalp of all, Viv Richards.

DON MOSEY *And we'll all be very interested to see if he can resist the temptation to hook early in the innings, before he's got a sight of the ball, the pace of the pitch and the bounce. Dilley will no doubt tempt him at the* *first opportunity. He bowls it — and he's out caught! Caught at slip by Botham. And the West Indies — put in — are 25 for two.*

Jackman then had Desmond Haynes caught behind for 25 and when Botham trapped the Jamaican Everton Mattis, playing in his second Test, lbw it was 65 for four.

The ball moved around and the West Indies were in trouble. Had it not been for a couple of mistakes by David Bairstow behind the wicket when the West Indies had lost those first four wickets, it would have been much worse. Bairstow dropped Larry Gomes and then missed stumping him and Gomes and Lloyd led a recovery.

TONY COZIER

Messrs Lloyd and Gomes added 154 runs for the fifth wicket, completely transforming the match. Lloyd reached his 100, but was out for exactly that, caught at square-leg off Jackman in the last hour of the day. Gomes, too, had fallen by the close, caught at slip off Dilley, who also picked up the wicket-keeper, David Murray. If England were pleased with the seven West Indies wickets they had taken on that first day for 238, they must have been relieved to take the last three quickly on the second morning — all three to Ian Botham. 265 was not a huge score, but it remained to be seen what England could do on that pitch. The openers were Graham Gooch and Geoff Boycott.

Boycott was extremely suspicious about the pitch. He came out the day before the match — Barbados had always been a very happy hunting ground for him — and the Barbados pitch had changed in the interim. So, instead of a bare, flat, batsman's pitch, which he'd always seen, he saw a pitch which was obviously better grassed than he'd ever seen before. My brother-in-law oversees the preparation of the pitch and he said he was there, leaning over the pitch when he heard this voice roaring behind him, 'What's the meaning of this, then?' It was the voice of Geoff Boycott.

TONY COZIER

Gooch faced the first over of the innings from Andy Roberts, making 6. Now Michael Holding marked out his run and prepared to bowl the second over to Geoff Boycott. A cricket drama was about to fill the stage.

The Boycott over from Holding has gone down as a cricket legend in the West Indies. It is repeated over and over. People who were not there will tell you exactly

Test   Match   Special

103

what happened with every ball and claim they were there. It was an outstanding over, there is no question about it. Here was one of the great opening batsmen of all time facing one of the greatest fast bowlers of all time. Holding just steamed in and gave him this tremendous over. I don't think he touched any delivery, even though he played at all.

TONY COZIER

It's a case of 'Spot the ball, Geoffrey' as a hostile Michael Holding casts a mesmerising spell over the England opener

TONY COZIER *And here is Holding coming in again from the northern end. On the way now to bowl to Boycott and Boycott is bowled! Leg stump out of the ground. A ball of full length. Boycott not in behind it and the leg stump plucked out of the ground and sent back a long, long way, almost towards the keeper. There are about four spectators on the ground now who*

cannot contain themselves who have rushed on to the ground to shake the hand of Holding as Boycott is bowled without scoring. The crowd jumping all over the place and what an over from Michael Holding. Boycott was nowhere in behind that at all. It was a ball of full length and it plucked his leg stump out of the ground and sent it reeling back.

Boycott was out to the final ball of Holding's over; an over which had taken everyone's breath away. The new batsman, Mike Gatting, was caught at slip in the next over from Roberts and it was 11 for two. Gooch and Gower took the score up to 40, before Gooch played a ball from Joel Garner onto his stumps. That at least brought a great moment for one England player. Roland Butcher, born in Barbados, had appropriately in that match become the first black West Indian born player to represent England in a Test match. His moment of glory was not to last too long, though. Like David Gower, he was caught in the slips off Colin Croft for 17. Botham added 22 runs for the sixth wicket with the gritty Peter Willey. It was time for Lloyd to make a change.

DON MOSEY *A bowling change which will not delight the eyes of the England batsmen any more or less than any has done so far, Michael Holding taking over from Joel Garner and he's on his way in. Botham . . . is dropped by the wicket-keeper! Beaten by Holding's first ball there, it was a magnificent delivery, arrowing in from wide of the off-stump. Botham changed his mind about the shot, finally dabbed down to protect his off-stump and the ball flew towards first slip, Murray got in the way, hands high, and the ball was deflected over the top of both Lloyd and Richards, first and second slips, and that one really took off. He's on his way in, bowls and again it takes off and whistles, and flew across the front of Botham's face. Botham gives a gesture of disgust, throws down his bat and comes down the pitch to talk to Peter Willey and the crowd don't think much of that. You get out of this wicket what you put into it and Holding puts everything into it. And here he goes again, bowls and this from shorter, a shorter length is still lifting into the rib cage of Ian Botham and as I've said Botham is not a man to show any reluctance at any stage. He's a very tough guy indeed and we've got the two toughest men in the England side together here at the moment and it's a little unnerving for anyone because this is great fast bowling at its very peak and Holding, knowing that he's got the batsmen wondering where the ball is going to fly, now comes in with a great spring in his step. In, bowls to Botham and drops this short and he's caught! That hit the glove. Caught by Murray at the second attempt and Botham plainly disgusted with the whole effort retires, caught Murray, bowled Holding for 26 and England are 94 for six.*

Ian Botham returned to the pavilion and quietly and sadly said to the cricket manager, Ken Barrington, that bowling like that was too much, even for him. The poignancy of such a conversation lies not so much in the fact that Holding's bowling was too hot for Botham to handle as that this would be the last day's cricket that Ken would see. That night, after England had collapsed to Holding, Roberts and Croft, Ken Barrington, veteran of many defiant innings for England, died of a heart attack.

I remember seeing Ken Barrington during that innings in that cosy little pavilion, and every wicket was a blow to him personally. Ken was a marvellous man. He was not a manager who harked back to the cricket of his day. He had the respect of the players, and no-one admired or loved him more than Ian Botham. Ken took their successes and failures very much to heart. I remember a ghastly moment when the news came through that Ken had died. Everybody was feeling desperately sad, and I thought England did remarkably well not to drop their bundle more than they did.

The atmosphere was one of stunned bemusement. We all felt as though we had lost a brother or someone close to our families. Ken was such a friend to all of us — he never had any animosity towards the Press. Ken would either answer questions or simply say that he did not want to answer them, but he never messed you about.

HENRY BLOFELD

Ken Barrington, seen here in the nets just a few weeks before the fateful third Test

DON MOSEY *Good morning. As many listeners will have heard Ken Barrington, the assistant manager of the England touring team in the West Indies, died late last night. This came as a sudden and dreadful shock to the entire touring party because Barrington, one of the most distinguished of post-war English batsmen who played in 82 Tests, scored 6,800 Test runs, was a very much loved man and now here on the Kensington Oval in Bridgetown, Barbados, a little tribute is to be paid to him. The England and the West Indies players have lined up in front of the pavilion. Along with them are Alec Bedser, for so long a colleague of Ken Barrington on the English selectors' panel, and Charlie Elliot another colleague in that department. There's Don Wilson, the MCC head coach at Lord's, and A C Smith the manager, stands at the head of the ranks. Alec Bedser and Charlie Elliot are now joined by Donald Carr, the Secretary of the Test and County Cricket Board and here is Mr Peter Short, President of the Barbados Cricket Association:*

PETER SHORT *'I must announce that last night the former England cricketer and assistant manager of the England team, Mr Ken Barrington, died very suddenly.'*

DON MOSEY *That's Mr Short making the announcement to the crowd, most of whom will be completely unaware of this news. Mr Short is offering the* *deepest and heartfelt sympathy to his wife Anne who is here with Ken, who has been with him for the last fortnight, and was with him when he died in his hotel room about 11.30 last evening. Mr Short offers his sympathies to the manager and members of the team and is now going to ask everyone in this ground to stand and observe a moment's silence. This ground is absolutely packed. It is now absolutely silent and all around the spectators stand. It's a very impressive sight and a very moving tribute to a very much loved cricketer. And now a moment of respect for Ken Barrington.*

It was the Sunday morning, the third day of the Test, and Ken Barrington would have been proud of the way they bowled and fielded that day, which started with the West Indies 6 for one, having lost Greenidge the previous evening as they started to build on the first innings lead of 143. But although they were never allowed to dominate totally, the West Indies kept accumulating. Colin Croft, who had come in as night-watchman, made 33, Haynes 25 and Mattis 24. Two wickets for Jackman and one for Botham saw them back into the pavilion, but the incoming Viv Richards was in determined mood after his first innings duck.

The England team stand in silence as a tribute to cricket manager, Ken Barrington

Test Match Special

*H*e has never really done all that well in Barbados, especially against Barbados, and he came out and he showed what he can do in that innings. The West Indies were ahead; they were looking to turn the screw — and Richards did it.

T O N Y C O Z I E R

TONY COZIER *87 for three. Dilley again comes in now to Richards. Short and Richards hooks. It's going to be . . . it's gone out of the ground I think. It's gone right over the Kensington stand and even at that he seemed to hit it with one hand. Short ball, and Richards got under it and lifted it right over the top of the Kensington stand and it finished up in a building site outside the ground. It was on its way to the deep water harbour but there are a few buildings in the way.*

Richards added 82 for the fifth wicket with Gomes, who eventually ran himself out for 34 and the excitement for the crowd was then whether he would reach his hundred before the close of that third day. He made it off the penultimate ball.

DON MOSEY *And Dilley moves in. Bowling to Richards. Richards swings it away over the square-leg boundary, four runs. And the crowds invade the ground. Scores and scores of boys come from two directions and 20 or 30*

Viv Richards more than made up for his first innings duck when he smashed a brilliant unbeaten 182 in the second innings to give West Indies an unassailable lead

Test Match Special

policemen out of the pavilion and they all meet in mid-pitch. Richards is engulfed by cheering youngsters, dancing, waving their arms and the policemen now arrive.

Over the rest day that followed, Clive Lloyd made it clear that his aim was a lead of 500 and on the fourth morning he and Richards set about getting it. Now they really did cut loose, particularly Richards. When the declaration came at lunch he was 182 not out. He and Lloyd had added 153 in only 136 minutes for the sixth wicket, before Botham had Lloyd lbw for 66. When he did close the innings at 379 for seven it left England five sessions of play to make 523 or, more realistically, to survive. Michael Holding again made a great impact with his first over of the innings, finishing it with a lifter that had Boycott caught in the gully for one and one that kept low to bowl Gatting first ball. But at 2 for two Graham Gooch was joined by David Gower. Refusing to be dominated by the West Indian bowling, they played their shots, adding 120 together before the gentle off-spin of Richards induced Gower to play the ball onto his stumps for 54. Richards also had Butcher lbw for 2 and Roberts had Botham caught at slip for 1, so that the hopes of salvation which were just budding at 122 for two had faded at 139 for five. But Gooch was still there and at the close he was 88, with England 166 for five. On the final morning Gooch got to his hundred.

REDS PEREIRA *Holding bowls to Gooch and that's turned away off the pads and that's Gooch's hundred. Out towards square-leg. He's back for the second, Mattis picks up now and Gooch turning that ball out from the leg stump. On comes an England supporter. He has not had too much to cheer, dressed in an off-colour white, dark shorts, shakes the hands of Gooch, taps him on the back. He has caused no harm and Gooch is 100. The West Indies team applauding, so are the crowd here at Kensington...five for 179.*

Graham Gooch made an heroic hundred during which his cover driving off the fast bowlers was remarkable. I think it was a far better innings than his 333 against India at Lord's in 1990.

HENRY BLOFELD

If Gooch, bouyed up by that hundred, believed that he and Willey had the saving of the match, that belief was cruelly shattered in one over from Croft in which Willey was given out lbw as he advanced down the pitch and Bairstow was caught behind. Croft it was, too, who ended all possible hope for England with the wicket of Gooch, caught at gully for 116. Though the tail hung around for a while, the West Indian celebrations of a 298 run victory were not long delayed. There followed a drawn Test match in Antigua to secure the series for the West Indies.

Test Match Special

Antigua was not so much a Test match as a celebration and a great occasion. It was the first Test match ever staged in Antigua, the home of Vivian Richards and Andy Roberts. Before the match Richards got married. There was a big wedding celebration and reception and he himself graced the occasion with an inevitable century. If the West Indies had won, it would have put the icing on the wedding cake.

TONY COZIER

Undefeated hundreds by Peter Willey in the first innings and Geoff Boycott in the second had secured the draw at least in that Fourth Test. The final match of the series was in Jamaica.

England were given the most tremendous start after being put in by the West Indies when Graham Gooch hit 153 out of a total of 285, another wonderful innings. He has now played so many of these dominating innings when no-one else was scoring, that there can be no doubt that Gooch is a great player.

I remember Holding bowling very well that day. He was a great sight running in to bowl, particularly at his home ground of Sabina Park. It was a battle of high technical skill between Holding and Gooch — master craftsman against master craftsman — and every ball was a thrill.

There were a lot of bouncers, but one was not so aware of them because Gooch was playing such a commanding innings. If a batsman can stand up to fast bowling and play the hook, it makes the bowler think twice. And it is the most thrilling sight in the world when a batsman hooks a fast bowler.

HENRY BLOFELD

Michael Holding, in his home island took five for 56 in an England innings of 285, which would have been a total collapse without Gooch's 153. Greenidge and Haynes then put on 116 for the first West Indies wicket — Greenidge 62 and Haynes 84. There were nineties from Lloyd and Gomes in the total of 442. That gave them a lead of 157, which looked decisive when the first three England batsmen were out for 32 in the second innings.

Just when it seemed everything was lost, David Gower came in and played an enigmatic innings of 154 in seven hours. He can do it, as he showed at the Oval in 1990, but why not more often and only when the chips are down? I don't know, and I'm sure it would take the psychiatrist's chair to explain David Gower. A wonderful player, he was in total control all of the time in that innings, with those lovely fluid off-drives.

This match was memorable for England because of the spirit the players showed at the end of the tour when they had been utterly demoralised by the quick bowling and then by poor Ken Barrington's death. They never had the slightest chance of winning a match, but they did very well to get out of the last two Tests with two draws.

HENRY BLOFELD

Gower and Willey put on 136 for the fourth wicket over the fourth and fifth days. Willey made 67 and Gower was 154 not out of England's 302 for six when the match was drawn. While scarcely an England triumph, it was at least a more defiant way for England to end that troubled series. Their captain, Ian Botham, had made only 73 runs in the four Tests, though he had at least been the leading England wicket taker with 15. He would dearly have liked to show West Indians the sort of performances that have rocked other countries.

I think West Indians saw Botham's outstanding all-round record as having been gained perhaps against lesser opponents, especially during the Packer years. Still, everyone knew he had it in him to turn Test matches and he had done it in the past, but he'd never really done it against the West Indies. But in that regard they looked on Ian Botham almost as a kindred spirit. He does have that kind of aggressive attitude which West Indians appreciate. But as far as his record goes, they did believe it was exaggerated.

TONY COZIER

FINAL · SCORES

Kensington Oval, Barbados, Third Test

WEST INDIES - First Innings

C G Greenidge, c Gooch b Jackman		14
D L Haynes, c Bairstow b Jackman		25
I V A Richards, c Botham b Dilley		0
E H Mattis, lbw b Botham		16
C H Lloyd, c Gooch b Jackman		100
H A Gomes, c Botham b Dilley		58
D A Murray, c Bairstow b Dilley		9
A M E Roberts, c Bairstow b Botham		14
J Garner, c Bairstow b Botham		15
M A Holding, c Gatting b Botham		0
C E H Croft, not out		0
Extras (b4, lb6, w2, nb2)		14
Total		265

Fall of wickets: 1-24, 2-25, 3-47, 4-65, 5-219, 6-224, 7-236, 8-258, 9-258, 10-265
Bowling: Dilley 23-7-51-3, Botham 25.1-5-77-4, Jackman 22-4-65-3, Emburey 18-4-45-0, Gooch 2-0-13-0

ENGLAND - First Innings

G A Gooch, b Garner		26
G Boycott, b Holding		0
M W Gatting, c Greenidge b Roberts		2
D I Gower, c Mattis b Croft		17
R O Butcher, c Richards b Croft		17
I T Botham, c Murray b Holding		26
P Willey, not out		19
D L Bairstow, c Mattis b Holding		0
J E Emburey, c Lloyd b Roberts		0
R D Jackman, c Roberts b Croft		7
G R Dilley, c Gomes b Croft		0
Extras (b1, lb1, nb6)		8
Total		122

Fall of wickets: 1-6, 2-11, 3-40, 4-55, 5-72, 6-94, 7-94, 8-97, 9-122, 10-122
Bowling: Roberts 11-3-29-2, Holding 11-7-16-3, Croft 13.5-2-39-4, Garner 12-5-30-1

WEST INDIES - Second Innings

C G Greenidge, lbw b Dilley		0
D L Haynes, lbw b Botham		25
I V A Richards, not out		182
E H Mattis, c Butcher b Jackman		24
C H Lloyd, lbw b Botham		66
H A Gomes, run out		34
D A Murray, not out		5
A M E Roberts, c Bairstow b Botham		0
C E H Croft, c Boycott b Jackman		33
Extras (b3, lb7)		10
Total (7 wkts)		379

Fall of wickets: 1-0, 2-57, 3-71, 4-130, 5-212, 6-365, 7-365
Bowling: Dilley 25-3-111-1, Botham 29-5-102-3, Jackman 25-5-76-2, Embury 24-7-57-0, Willey 6-0-23-0

ENGLAND · Second Innings

G A Gooch, c Garner b Croft		116
G Boycott, c Garner b Holding		1
M W Gatting, b Holding		0
D I Gower, b Richards		54
R O Butcher, lbw b Richards		2
I T Botham, c Lloyd b Roberts		1
P Willey, lbw b Croft		17
D L Bairstow, c Murray b Croft		2
J E Emburey, b Garner		9
R D Jackman, b Garner		7
G R Dilley, not out		7
Extras (b1, lb3, nb4)		8
Total		224

Fall of wickets: 1-2, 2-2, 3-122, 4-134, 5-139, 6-196, 7-198, 8-201, 9-213, 10-224
Bowling: Roberts 20-6-42-1, Holding 19-6-46-2, Croft 19-1-65-3, Garner 16.2-6-39-2, Richards 17-6-24-2

West Indies won by 298 runs

FINAL · SCORES

Sabina Park, Kingston, Fifth Test

ENGLAND - First innings

G A Gooch, c Murray b Holding	153
G Boycott, c Murray b Garner	40
C W J Athey, b Holding	3
D Gower, b Croft	22
P Willey, c Murray b Marshall	4
R Butcher, b Garner	32
I T Botham, c Greenidge b Marshall	13
P R Downton, c Croft b Holding	0
J E Emburey, b Holding	1
R D Jackman, c Haynes b Holding	0
G R Dilley, not out	1
Extras (b8, nb8)	16
Total	285

Fall of wickets: 1-93, 2-148, 3-196, 4-210, 5-249, 6-275, 7-283, 8-283, 9-284
Bowling: Holding 18-3-56-5, Marshall 16-2-49-2, Croft 17-4-92-1, Garner 20-4-43-2, Richards 12-2-29-0

WEST INDIES - First innings

C G Greenidge, c Botham b Dilley	62
D L Haynes, b Willey	84
I V A Richards, c Downton b Dilley	15
E H Mattis, c sub b Dilley	34
C H Lloyd, c Downton b Jackman	95
H A Gomes, not out	90
D A Murray, c Gooch b Emburey	14
M D Marshall, b Emburey	15
J Garner, c sub b Dilley	19
M A Holding, c Downton b Botham	0
C E H Croft, c sub b Botham	0
Extras (lb8, nb5, w1)	14
Total	442

Fall of wickets: 1-116. 2-136, 3-179, 4-227, 5-345, 6-372, 7-415, 8-441, 9-442
Bowling: Dilley 28.4-6-116-4, Botham 26.1-9-73-2, Jackman 26.2-6-57-1, Gooch 8-3-20-0, Emburey 56-23-108-2, Willey 18-3-54-1

ENGLAND - Second innings

G A Gooch, c Lloyd b Marshall	3
G Boycott, c Garner b Croft	12
C W J Athey, c Murray b Holding	1
D I Gower, not out	154
P Willey, c Greenidge b Richards	67
R O Butcher, lbw b Croft	0
I T Botham, c Garner b Holding	16
P R Downton, not out	26
Extras (b6, lb13, nb4)	23
Total (6 wkts dec)	302

Fall of wickets: 1-5, 2-10, 3-32, 4-168, 5-168, 6-215
Bowling: Holding 28-7-58-2, Marshall 5-0-15-1, Croft 29-7-80-2, Garner 24-7-46-0, Richards 23-8-48-1, Gomes 13-3-18-0, Mattis 5-1-10-0, Haynes 1-0-4-0

Match drawn

Showing defiance in the face of adversity, Graham Gooch hit 116 out of a total of 224 in Bridgetown, but even his superhuman effort could not save the match for England

Test Match Special

1984 Lord's and Headingley

SECOND TEST, 28-30 JUNE, 2, 3 JULY

THIRD TEST, 12-14, 16 JULY

Commentators: BRIAN JOHNSTON, HENRY BLOFELD, TONY COZIER,
TONY LEWIS, CHRISTOPHER MARTIN-JENKINS, DON MOSEY
Summarisers: TREVOR BAILEY, FRED TRUEMAN, MIKE DENNESS,
RAY ILLINGWORTH

In 1984 the England players who had taken part in a tour of South Africa in 1982, among them Graham Gooch, John Emburey, Geoff Boycott and Derek Underwood, were in the third and final year of a Test and County Cricket Board ban from international cricket. Their absence had cleared the way immediately for the selection of the South African-born Allan Lamb. In the meantime the settled West Indies team had, if anything, become even stronger.

The first Test of the series was at Edgbaston, where David Gower led England for the first time in his own right, rather than as a stand-in for the injured Bob Willis. It was not a happy start for him. England were bundled out, principally by Joel Garner, for 191 and their new cap, Andy Lloyd, was hit on the head by Malcolm Marshall and rendered incapable of playing again that season. The West Indies replied with hundreds from Larry Gomes and Viv Richards and, when England thought they were through the batting at 455 for eight, 87 not out from Eldine Baptiste and 69 from Michael Holding to take them to 606. Garner took nine wickets and the West Indies won by an innings and 180 runs.

For the second Test at Lord's, the replacement opener for Andy Lloyd was another new cap, Chris Broad, and he and Graeme Fowler gave England a splendid start, putting on 101 for the first wicket, before Broad was caught behind off Marshall for 55. Before the close of the first day, England had also lost Gower, lbw to Marshall for 3. But it was an encouraging first day with England, only too happy that the West Indies were without the injured Holding, ending it at 167 for two.

The second day started with the early dismissals of Lamb for 23 and Gatting for 1. Both were lbw to Marshall, and Gatting brought plenty of opprobrium on himself for padding up to the ball that got him out.

CHRISTOPHER MARTIN-JENKINS *Gatting, in fact, averaging 58 this season, looks round at the ground which is so very familiar to him, twirls the bat a* *couple of times and one hopes that the atmosphere of a full Lord's will inspire him as Chris Broad said it inspired him yesterday. Marshall turns, runs in at an angle, gathering speed and bowls smoothly to Gatting who pads up and he's lbw. He pads up, not playing a stroke and that is the way that he's been out so often. Thrusting the front leg forward, it was certainly outside the line of the off-stump, but Mike Gatting seems all too often to disregard the fact that that lbw law has been changed and that a batsman may be given out if he doesn't play a stroke and in the opinion of the umpire the ball would have come back and hit the stumps. It'll be interesting to see the replay of that but a crestfallen Mike Gatting, to the disappointment I'm sure of all English followers and certainly of the Middlesex ones, is lbw to Marshall for one. Malcolm Marshall has now taken all four England wickets and England are 185 for four.*

Graeme Fowler, with determination and courage and not without the odd flirtation outside his off stump, reached a well-deserved hundred, before Baptiste had him caught in the gully for 106. Baptiste also got Botham after he had contributed some lusty blows in making 30. Paul Downton provided some staunch defence, as he had at Edgbaston, making 23 not out, but after such a good start, England's total of 286 was disappointing. Malcolm Marshall had risen to the occasion by taking a marvellous six for 85.

Ian Botham had never really enjoyed the greatest success against the West Indies, but he started now with the new ball as if he was determined to put all that right. Gordon Greenidge was caught at slip for 1 and Desmond Haynes lbw for 12. It was 18 for two with the two Edgbaston century-makers, Gomes and Richards together. But Botham was not finished.

CHRISTOPHER MARTIN-JENKINS *Three slips, gully and two short-legs go down as Botham comes in, round the wicket, bowls to the left-handed Gomes who's hit on the pad and a catch is it? Yes, he's out, caught off bat and pad. Brilliantly caught too by Mike Gatting at forward short-leg. Gomes played at that. The umpire deciding that the ball had hit an inside edge, gone on to the pad and Gatting, diving forward at forward short, rather as he did on several occasions against Australia in 1981, took a very good right-handed catch at full stretch an inch from the ground. Gomes walks out with his runner Gordon Greenidge, looking a little unhappy with life and possibly might have felt he didn't hit it or it may just be that he's disappointed to get out cheaply, injured as well and looking up at the scoreboard, 35 for three, things not*

**Graeme Fowler on his
way to a brave 106**

Test Match Special

115

going too well for the West Indies but splendidly for England. Well what a scene is set now because we've got two of the greatest of all modern West Indies batsmen, Clive Lloyd, coming out to join Viv Richards with their side in trouble, a full Lord's, sun shining. You really couldn't ask for a situation more pregnant with possibilities than that.

Ian Botham had taken all three wickets, but there were to be no more for him on that second day, as Richards and Lloyd carried the West Indies total past a hundred and were still there at the close, having added 84 already and either or both of them looking likely to grace a Lord's Saturday with a century. But Botham nipped such thoughts in the bud by having his old friend Richards adjudged lbw, a decision which aroused considerable controversy when the umpire, Barrie Meyer, admitted later that he might have made a mistake. It was a match of lbws, equalling the world record for a Test match, and, after Richards had gone for 72, his partner in that fourth wicket stand of 103, Clive Lloyd, was also lbw to Botham for 39. Botham was now inspired and was to continue his bowling spell for the rest of the innings, getting Dujon for 8. But England were held up by some strokeplay from Baptiste with 44 and Marshall with 29. Bob Willis ended both those innings, but it was Botham who finished matters off.

BRIAN JOHNSTON *He's running in from the Nursery end now to bowl to Garner. Garner just plays that one outside. He's nicked it. He's caught again well in front of first slip by Downton, a good falling catch. Garner caught Downton, bowled Botham for six. West Indies are all out for 245 and that means that Botham has got his eight wickets and now needs five to take 300 wickets and Garner walks back. Milton Small is not out three, which will improve his batting average in his career, and naturally enough Botham is going to be shoved forward by the side to take the cheers from the crowd who are standing to him. You don't often see people taking eight wickets. We did see Massie take eight wickets at Lord's here. And Botham being very modest but Gower waiting and letting Botham lead the England side in, as of course he did when he was captain here before, but now he goes because he's taken these eight wickets. England lead by 41.*

Botham had taken eight for 103, but that 41-run lead was soon made to look rather paltry as Chris Broad, batting with a groin strain, was an early victim of Garner, for a duck. Then Milton Small removed the two left-handers, Fowler and Gower, with the score still in the thirties. Lamb and Gatting added 52, but Gatting seemed to have learned nothing from his first innings dismissal and again padded up to Marshall to be lbw, this time for 29. England were 88 for four with only just over half the game gone — 129 ahead. Botham joined Lamb and they added another 26 runs before the close. They had to wait to resume their partnership for some rain on the fourth morning, but when they did, as the West Indies tried to defend their position, they started to put on a substantial stand. Botham was already only five short of three hundred Test wickets and now he reached a batting milestone.

HENRY BLOFELD *Here now is Marshall again from the Nursery end. He is starting his eighteenth over. Up to the wicket, bowls to Botham. Botham drives. Four runs. He hit that on the up. It went away like a guided missile. It hit the fencing there in front of the Mound Stand, bounced about five yards back and, honestly, no one had moved before it had hit the fencing. What a stroke! What a stroke, Trevor!*

TREVOR BAILEY *That was probably the best stroke, I would say without doubt, the best stroke we've seen in this match and we've seen some pretty good ones. That really was rather special because he hit it on the up, along the ground and it just sort of went roaring past cover, in between cover and extra cover and no-one really moved.*

BILL FRINDALL *And with that stroke he reached the landmark of 4,000 runs in Test cricket.*

Lamb and Botham put on 128 for the fifth wicket, replacing the ball firmly in England's court.

HENRY BLOFELD *Vivian Richards folding his hands across his chest with his cap on his head, has rather the air of someone who's seen it all before and I dare say he has, except it's unusual for him playing for the West Indies to be on the side that's not doing so well. As Garner bowls again to Botham. Comes forward. There's an appeal for lbw. He's out. He's lbw. He's out. Botham's innings has ended lbw, bowled Garner for 81. He came forward. He was hit, I thought, fairly low down on the pad. Botham looks to me as though he's not entirely happy. Umpire Evans thought about it then raised his left finger and Botham's splendid innings has come to an end. 216 for five. Botham lbw, bowled Garner 81. He takes his crash helmet off and just listen to the applause.*

Fourteen more runs were added after Botham's departure before Downton was lbw to Small for 4, so it was Geoff Miller who was with Allan Lamb when he reached his first hundred against the West Indies.

BRIAN JOHNSTON *And Marshall wiping sweat off his brow on to the ball. And away he goes now, his shadow just to his right. Lamb on 99 waiting here as Marshall comes up, bowls to him and he's cut that one. That's it. He's cut that for four down to backward point and Lamb has made a hundred, a very welcome one to him, back in the runs in Test cricket and he is 103 not out and England are 273 for six, and one or two people I'm afraid running on to congratulate him. What a splendid innings by Allan*

Lamb. The end of that over and one or two of the stewards have come and taken the people off who were coming to clap the batsman on the back. In fact Lamb's being shaken by the hand by all sorts of people out there, including Dujon the wicket-keeper which is nice. 273 for six, then.
RAY ILLINGWORTH *Well that was a particularly good innings from Allan Lamb. He hasn't been in particularly good nick, even in county cricket he's had to struggle a bit lately, but he's certainly concentrated exceedingly hard throughout this innings and he's played very well indeed.*

Allan Lamb reaches his first hundred against West Indies as Clive Lloyd applauds

Miller was bowled by Harper for 9, but with a lead now past three hundred the onlookers expected England to be going for quick runs and a declaration that evening. But as play entered the last hour of the fourth day there was more controversy.

CHRISTOPHER MARTIN-JENKINS *The umpires are offering them, or going to offer them the light I think.*
TREVOR BAILEY *And the worry from Gower's point of view . . . I mean he would obviously like to think in terms of a declaration but I've got a feeling that the light is going to get too dark. They'll go on batting, yes.*
CHRISTOPHER MARTIN-JENKINS *Well I hope so. I wouldn't bank on it knowing . . . They must go on, please.*
TREVOR BAILEY *Well if they go, if they come off for bad light, the batsmen, they'll be, I mean they'll be simply mad.*
CHRISTOPHER MARTIN-JENKINS *Lamb is looking at the umpires as though he's longing for them to offer it to them. Pringle is out there. I don't know whether they've looked up at David Gower for instructions. Now David Evans is having a look and they're coming off, would you believe it? And the Lord's crowd are appalled at that, and with good reason, because England have got a chance of winning this game and they appear now to be throwing it away because time is of the essence if they're going to bowl the West Indies out. They've got three good wickets left. They've got a lead of, at this moment, 328 runs and here they are with an hour's play left, just under an hour's play left, and now they are going to waste a great chance of getting runs on the board.*
TREVOR BAILEY *Well it's . . . It doesn't make any sense at all.*
CHRISTOPHER MARTIN-JENKINS *Except the West Indies will be delighted to come off.*
TREVOR BAILEY *Oh yes, not half. The only thing that could be said is that they've reduced the length of the match and therefore their chances of being defeated — I think their chances of being defeated were fairly remote anyway, what it really means is that England have decreased their chances of winning, which seems to me rather stupid.*

David Gower surveys the scene from the England dressing room balcony. Controversy surrounded his decision to summon the England batsmen to come off for bad light

There was a great hoo-ha in the papers on the last morning when all sorts of accusations were made against David Gower. Someone said he had been watching television and could not give a damn about what was going on out in the middle and that he should have declared and given his bowlers a chance to get a wicket or two before the end.

TONY COZIER

After the premature end on the Monday evening, England batted on for another twenty minutes next morning to get the score up to 300, losing Lamb for 110 and Pringle for 9 in the process. The West Indies had five and a half hours to survive, or a target of 342 if they were interested.

Test Match Special

119

No team would have been expected to make the 342 runs. I had been invited to lunch in the MCC President's box with a number of Caribbean High Commissioners and, rather facetiously, I said there, 'It's going to be a piece of cake and the West Indies should be winning this well within time.' Of course I was only leg pulling and never honestly thought that the West Indies would get up to win the match.

TONY COZIER

With the score 57 and the West Indies clearly now looking more than a little interested in the target, Haynes was run out for 17. Larry Gomes came in to join Gordon Greenidge, who was starting to show off his range of attacking strokes.

Greenidge was quite unstoppable and in magnificent form, but I don't think we should forget the vital role that Larry Gomes played at the other end. It was an outstanding season for Gomes. He was a very unobtrusive left-hander and the support he gave to Greenidge was absolutely crucial. It also helped that he was a left-hander and the England bowlers could not quite adjust to the left-handed/right-handed combination.

TONY COZIER

You would have thought the safest bet was a draw, but this man, Gordon Greenidge, turned England's bowling upside down and gave them a hiding they would not want to remember. There was some very wayward bowling by the England attack and he was cutting and pulling and hooking all day.

FRED TRUEMAN

BRIAN JOHNSTON *Away goes Willis to bowl to Greenidge. Greenidge 99. Faces up to Willis. Is this it? No, he plays forward there and it goes out in to the off-side and is fielded by Gower. So the crowd having plenty to enjoy and they've seen some lovely strokeplay today, England going on for another 20 minutes, or 19 minutes, this morning and now West Indies chasing this target of 342, going great guns. And they'll have a lot to thank Greenidge for. 99. I suggest he may get one down to long leg this ball, if it's on his leg stump he might tickle it down to Broad, we shall see. Willis running in. Greenidge 99, waits for him. Up comes Willis, past umpire Barry Meyer. Bowls this one and it's outside the off-stump and goes through low to Downton. No stroke offered by Greenidge. Downton has kept wicket impeccably as far as I'm concerned. They haven't all been easy,*

Gordon Greenidge hooks during his magnificent 214 not out

some balls have kept a bit low there which are rather nasty to take. And he caught two very good catches. Willis makes his way back. Always an effort for him, one feels, to come back for a second spell but he's doing it valiantly. He's running in now, down the track, his feet in exactly the same places as he comes up now. Bowls to Greenidge on 99. Greenidge cuts this one and this is going to be it. It goes to Fowler but he's deeper this time. Greenidge gets his 100, his hands up in the air, the bat in the air. He takes his cap off. No-one, thank goodness, has run on to congratulate him but we all applaud him from here and so do the crowd. A very fine hundred. The West Indies are 149 for one.

TREVOR BAILEY *Yes it was a splendid 100 but we've now seen Willis bowling, that over only conceded two runs and if he goes on bowling like that it's going to make life extremely difficult because Willis isn't easy to hit, not normally, not with a defensive field which he's got now but of*

T e s t   M a t c h   S p e c i a l

course he's got to be able to come back, not for the second spell, for the third spell because that's going to be the crucial one. England now can slow the over rate down considerably but not for the last hour, when you've got to bowl the 20 overs.

At 110, Greenidge was missed at slip off Willis, but he continued to dispel any lingering doubts that the West Indies would reach their goal. As it became a formality, he reached his double century in which he had faced only 232 balls and hit two sixes and twenty-eight fours.

TONY COZIER *Gordon Greenidge has set up this victory with an innings of 214 in which he has hammered the ball all over the ground with complete assurance and confidence. Larry Gomes, the left hander, less powerful but no less effective, is 87.*

Ian Botham is going to bowl this over. He's going to bowl spin. Downton is up to the stumps. The West Indies need two more to win and let's see what he does. Ian Botham off two or three paces is bowling from the Pavilion End and he comes in now to Gomes and Gomes goes back and hits the winning runs through the off-side for four. The West Indies have won this match by nine wickets. 344 for one, having been set 342 to win. Gordon Greenidge finishes 214 not out. Larry Gomes is 92 not out. The West Indies go 2-0 up in the series with one of the most remarkable victories in the history of Test cricket. The crowd is swarming on to the ground. The West Indies have won the match with, in fact, 11 overs to go. So really a very convincing victory by this strong West Indies team. It's their fifth consecutive Test victory following the three against Australia in the West Indies in the recent series and the one in the First Test match here.

Godfrey Evans and Ian Botham congratulate Gordon Greenidge on his match-winning double century

Nine days after that staggering nine-wicket win at Lord's, the third Test started at Headingley. Mike Gatting had paid the penalty for his two extraordinary misjudgements in the second Test. A weight of opinion said that that must be his last chance. In thirty Tests he had yet to score a hundred. No one would have believed that in two years he would be captain of England. Now he made way for the third new batting cap of the series, Paul Terry of Hampshire. In the seam bowling department, Paul Allott replaced Neil Foster and the selectors changed from the off-spin of Geoff Miller to the slow left-arm variety of young Nick Cook from Northamptonshire.

Despite overcast conditions and England's perenniel mistrust of the Headingley pitch, Gower chose to bat first on winning the toss against an attack that now had Michael Holding restored to it — the only change from the Lord's team. By lunch three wickets had gone down cheaply and not long after it was 87 for four, when Broad was caught off Roger Harper for 32. One incident, at least, had made life a little less difficult for the England batsmen. Malcolm Marshall, when he had bowled only six overs, had been hit on the hand while fielding in the gully and had had to go off for treatment to what was revealed to be a fractured left thumb.

From 87 for four, Lamb and Botham started another partnership to steady England's ship. They had added 85 when Botham was caught behind off Baptiste for 45. But Allan Lamb continued towards his second Test century in successive innings.

DON MOSEY *Here comes Holding, that's a fairly swift one, lashed away forward of cover, there's little Logie in hot pursuit, he can't pick it up, the ball races over the boundary ropes by the dressing rooms and that was a very handsomely struck four taking Lamb on to 98 and England up to 234 for five. All eyes on Alan Lamb on 98. Holding to Lamb, Lamb gets a little tucked up, but Logie overruns the ball and it's going to give him his hundred. Logie coming in from cover tried to pick it up and throw at the stumps, took his eye off the ball for a moment, missed it, and Lamb holds up both arms to the dressing room and then takes off his helmet, which is rather a nice gesture to see these days because normally batsman wave their bats, which used to be the way of acknowledging applause when they were not wearing hats, it isn't often one sees them raise the hats. The crowd rise to him, Lamb 100 not out. It has come in 218 minutes off 178 balls and has included 15 fours.*

Lamb is so West Indian in his approach and attitude to batting and in his style. Having been reared under similar conditions in South Africa it is nothing more than you would expect, but his whole competitiveness won the respect of West Indians from this, his first series against the West

Test   Match   Special

*Indies. He seems to enjoy playing against them and there is
a grudging respect for the way he takes on the West Indies'
fast bowlers. He seems to enjoy it and not many do.*

TONY COZIER

There was only time after Lamb's hundred at the end of the first day for
Harper to dismiss Downton for 17 and one more run to be scored before
the close at 237 for six. The decline on the second morning was
disappointing for them. Lamb was out without adding to his 100 and
Holding cleaned up the tail to finish with four for 70 as England had to
settle for 270.

The early wicket of Gordon Greenidge for Bob Willis was the sort of
encouragement England needed and Paul Allott celebrated his recall after
two years by bowling Haynes for 18 and having Richards caught for 15.
It was 78 for three, but a left-handed partnership of Gomes and Lloyd
added 70 before Cook had Lloyd caught by his opposing captain for 48.
Dujon now stayed with Gomes while 53 runs were added and 200 was
passed, making England's first innings score look very vulnerable. But
Allott set the West Indies back on their heels with three quick wickets to
leave them 206 for seven.

Larry Gomes was still there and he was able to be largely a spectator
as his new partner, Michael Holding launched an assault which started
on the second evening and finished on the third morning, bringing him
59 runs in an eighth wicket stand of 82 and swept West Indies into the
lead. His wicket, hooking to fine leg, gave Bob Willis some revenge for
plenty of indignity suffered at his hands. With Joel Garner at the other
end, Larry Gomes was now in danger of running out of partners as he
neared his hundred.

TONY COZIER *Number 10 in the batting order, only number 10 because of
the fact that Malcolm Marshall is injured and will not bat, otherwise Joel
Garner would have been 11. Here comes Willis from the Kirkstall Lane
end to bowl to Gomes. Gomes forward, drives up on the on-side, they've
gone for one, a chase here from mid-off around to mid-on by Terry and
he's out! Run out! So Garner is run out and Larry Gomes is left not out 96
trying for a second run which was not there, even with Joel Garner coming
to the danger end as Paul Terry sent the return at the first bounce and no
matter how long the strides of Garner. Now, is Marshall going to come
out? Well they're waving, yes it looks as if he is going to come out. In fact
everyone was walking off and Malcolm Marshall will come out in the
interest of Larry Gomes getting a century. So Larry Gomes is 96 not out
and everybody was trooping off thinking it was the end of the innings and
in fact Marshall is going to come out. That's been the advice from the
dressing room. Looks as if he's had to change pretty quickly. There's a lot
of activity going on in that dressing room now, you can see it through the*

Malcolm Marshall defied the pain of a fractured left thumb and took on the England attack, hand in plaster

glass. He's apparently now got on all his gear, he's coming out, he's rushing down the steps, he didn't expect it, of course, but like Colin Cowdrey did on that famous occasion at Lord's in 1963 when he came out with two balls of the match remaining in the interest of saving the match for England, Malcolm Marshall now comes out on to the ground in the interest of his team-mate getting a century. Larry Gomes has got 96. He's just lost what everyone felt would have been his last partner Joel Garner, run out going for a second run. Garner run out without scoring at the non-strikers end and the umpire, in fact, David Constant, had taken the bails off and was walking

T e s t   M a t c h   S p e c i a l

back into the dressing room. The players were walking back into the dressing room. Malcolm Marshall, with his left hand in plaster, comes onto the ground to join Larry Gomes. Gomes comes out and has a word with Marshall, there are three balls left in the over and I wonder if they will expect Marshall to face a ball. I doubt it. 290 for nine, Gomes 96. Fielders go all the way back and now we'll soon know whether Malcolm Marshall's unselfish move will pay dividends. 96 to Gomes, he faces the bowling of Willis, pushes on the on-side. They go for one. They will look for a second. They'll have to hurry. Pringle is on to it now, over-runs the ball. They get the second run. Pushed it on the on-side, took off for one. It was always going to be a close second. Pringle not extremely fast in the field, came in, over-ran the ball and the batsmen got two to carry Gomes to 98. Two more balls left in the over. 292 for nine.

Here's Willis now coming in to Gomes who's 98. Gomes hits it over the top of the bowler's head and that's his century. He's got it. Four runs over the head of Willis. So Larry Gomes has got this richly deserved century. All the West Indian players, the manager, are on the dressing room balcony cheering loudly and quite visibly ensuring that Larry Gomes sees them so that he knows what they feel about his performance. This has been a superb innings by Gomes who has batted so well during the summer. He's 102 and Malcolm Marshall coming out at the non-strikers end to allow him to get the four runs he needed at the dismissal of Joel Garner. So he's got the century. It's the last ball of the over and I would say the last ball of the innings, of course, unless Larry Gomes gets a single. His century came in 299 minutes, 187 deliveries. He faces Willis now. He goes back and hooks down over mid-wicket. Back goes Gower and in fact two of them go back and the batsmen take a single and Pringle comes across and falls on his back, now getting up rather awkwardly from the turf and Gomes, really for the first time I can remember, hooking at a bouncer from Willis and getting the single which will give him the strike, so in fact there'll be no declaration. He's 103. The West Indies are 297 now for nine and Malcolm Marshall not yet having faced a ball, and I'm sure that when he does, or if he does, have the opportunity of facing one that the declaration will be made right away.

Here was Malcolm Marshall with his thumb all strapped up and a little way into the West Indies innings he said to Clive Lloyd that he felt he might be able to bat. Nobody took him seriously, but in the end he did go out to bat to give Larry Gomes a century.

TONY COZIER

DON MOSEY *Three balls in the over from Allott still to be bowled. Malcolm Marshall, with left hand in plaster, right hand more orthodoxly protected by a batting glove, faces Allott with three slips, a gully, a silly* *mid-off, a short square-leg and an orthodox point, and he'll just be content I think to shuffle forward and try to keep the ball out and give Gomes the strike when possible. Allott bowls and he takes one hand away, aims a big waft with the right hand, takes the left hand out of the way and fails to make any contact and there's a little, sympathetic round of applause for him for the fact that he's coming in. Botham is mightily amused by the whole thing, one can see his broad grin from here. So, it really requires a pitched up straight ball, Fred doesn't it?*

FRED TRUEMAN *I should think a yorker, straight, somewhere round about leg and middle would be enough to give Paul Allott a sixth wicket. I was amazed, actually, when I saw him take the hand off and waft at it with one hand but it poses the other question, if he's willing to bat, is he willing to bowl?*

DON MOSEY *Well, yes, good question. Allott in, bowls, and again this time one handed, he plays, Marshall plays it back to Allott and Allott striving for the straight ball, well pitched up there, achieved it but Marshall coming forward, again removing the left hand, playing it right-handed back to the bowler and the West Indies, after two interruptions for bad light this morning, are 298 for nine. During the morning they've lost Holding, caught Allott at long leg, bowled Willis for 59, a marvellously merry innings of five sixes and three fours off just 55 balls. And here's Allott to complete his over, bowling to the one handed Marshall who gets runs, through the gully and Terry is in pursuit. I don't think he'll beat that to the ropes. Some helpful youngster comes in, picks it up as it hits the ropes, lobs it back and Marshall is off the mark with four runs and Allott stands with his head downcast as much as to say 'Why can't I get out a man who's batting with one hand?'*

Allott eventually did end Marshall's outrageous one-handed flailing with a catch to second slip. The West Indies were all out for 302, 32 runs ahead, and Allott had taken six for 61.

Marshall had helped his team-mate get a hundred and everyone felt that that was enough from him — no more heroics. Then all of a sudden we saw him come out with this left hand strapped and ready to bowl and he actually opened the bowling. The hand was strapped with white plaster and the England batsmen complained that it was distracting them. Marshall then went to a plaster which was closer to flesh colour and he just ran through them. He swung the ball magnificently all over the place. It was more swing than pace. It really was a quite remarkable performance by a player who was quite seriously handicapped by his injury, although he did not seem so.

TONY COZIER

Test Match Special

127

TONY LEWIS *Marshall's active, coming in again. Bowls to Broad. Oh, it's popped. It's up in the air, it's an easy catch to backward short-leg and Marshall has got a wicket.*

After Broad had gone for two, there was another wicket before England were even half way to erasing the first innings deficit, when Garner had Terry lbw for 1. Gower, though, joined Fowler in a stand of 91, which made the position look a lot more prosperous, before Harper had Gower caught behind for 43 and then Marshall struck again.

Ignoring the discomfort to bowl as well, Malcolm Marshall took seven for 53 in the England second innings

TONY LEWIS *Fowler has done extremely well. He has fought it out, difficult moments early on when Joel Garner and Malcolm Marshall had the new ball. Never easy. In comes Marshall and forward goes . . . Oh, he's caught him! Caught and bowled! Forward defensive stroke by Fowler, very firmly played and with the one good hand. Malcolm Marshall takes an amazing reflex caught and bowled. Jubilation for the West Indies, tragedy for England, Graeme Fowler caught and bowled Marshall for 50 and the fourth wicket goes down for 106.*

Well it's been a remarkable day for Malcolm Marshall because no one expected him to bat first of all but then Garner got run out and we thought that's it, nine wickets down, no Marshall but West Indians came to the balcony and said stay out there. Gomes was then 96 not out. Gomes got to his century without Marshall facing a ball but he insisted and went on and played a couple of shots with the right hand only. In he comes now to bowl to Lamb, strikes him on the pad. How's that? That's out, lbw! Up go Marshall's hands and up run all his team-mates and sadly for Allan Lamb up went the finger of David Evans.

Botham and Downton had their sixth wicket stand of 28 terminated by Garner, who had Botham caught behind for 14, so that at the close of the third day England were 135 for six. As if he had not done enough that day the fourth day was to belong to the remarkable Marshall.

TONY LEWIS *In comes Marshall and it's a . . . it's a catch! A beautiful catch at first slip by Clive Lloyd. It's an incredible catch. I hesitated because Nick Cook went to play at the ball, then withdrew the bat and he slanted it downwards into the slip area, Richards dived across and obscured everything from view and Clive Lloyd rolled, rolled over, must have tucked his fingers underneath it and held a magnificent catch and no-one knew until Clive Lloyd himself emerged and threw it up. Well that was a wonderful catch. It's Marshall's fourth wicket and Cook was caught by Lloyd, bowled by Marshall for nought, England 138 for seven.*

Just two runs later and Malcolm Marshall was in the thick of things yet again for the West Indies.

TONY LEWIS *Every bit the start that West Indies wanted. Marshall building up this lovely bustling action and that strikes Pringle on the pad. He's out! Third ball, just a shuffling sort of shot, no shot at all really. And this ball instead of swinging away caught Pringle straight in front of the stumps and umpire David Evans had no hesitation. Five wickets to Marshall. The man with the doubly fractured left thumb. Well it is amazing, isn't it, and I'm sure Derek Pringle will be rather sad to be retreating, but lbw bowled Marshall two. England 140 for eight .*

There was no stopping the great fast bowler now, with the England tail well exposed.

TONY LEWIS *Marshall is in, bowls, and that strikes Allott on the pad. He's out lbw. It has to be right because Allott went right back on his stumps, the ball appeared to keep low. Umpire David Evans no hesitation, a formality. Paul Allott looked around slightly bemused, no sort of shot to a ball well up, and so Allott is lbw bowled by Marshall for four and England sadly 146 for nine.*

TONY COZIER *This is the seventh time in Tests that Marshall has taken five wickets or more in an innings and the second in this series. Six for 85 he had at Lord's and he's already had 17 wickets in this series. So here comes on the way now to Downton who drives. He is caught behind. That's the end of the England innings. Marshall's seventh wicket in the innings. England all out one fifty-nine. The West Indies need 128 to win the match and to take a three-nil lead in the series. So the first time that Malcolm Marshall has taken seven wickets in an innings and what a performance by the one-armed bandit, as he was being referred to in the press yesterday. Downton caught Dujon bowled Marshall 27. Willis is left not out five. It's 159 all out for England and we haven't even gone a half an hour into the day's play yet.*

Malcolm Marshall had bowled 26 overs, nine of them maidens, and had taken seven for 53.

One always wonders with Malcolm Marshall where the pace comes from, but to me he is in the top flight of fast bowling. He proved to me that he was head and shoulders above the rest in the MCC Bicentenary match.

FRED TRUEMAN

West Indies required 128 to win and achieved that easily with eight wickets to spare after a stand of 108 between Greenidge and Haynes.

Test   Match   Special

Test Match Special

FINAL · SCORES

Lord's, London, Second Test

ENGLAND - First Innings

G Fowler, c Harper b Baptiste	106
B C Broad, c Dujon b Marshall	55
D I Gower, lbw b Marshall	3
A J Lamb, lbw b Marshall	23
M W Gatting, lbw b Marshall	1
I T Botham, c Richards b Baptiste	30
P R Downton, not out	23
G Miller, run out	0
D R Pringle, lbw b Garner	2
N A Foster, c Harper b Marshall	6
R G D Willis, b Marshall	2
Extras (b4, lb14, w2, nb15)	35
Total	286

Fall of wickets: 1-101, 2-106, 3-183, 4-185, 5-243, 6-248, 7-251, 8-255, 9-264
Bowling: Garner 32-10-67-1, Small 9-0-38-0, Marshall 36.5-10-85-6, Baptiste 20-6-36-2, Harper 8-0-25-0

WEST INDIES - First Innings

C G Greenidge, c Miller b Botham	1
D L Haynes, lbw b Botham	12
H A Gomes, c Gatting b Botham	10
I V A Richards, lbw b Botham	72
C H Lloyd, lbw b Botham	39
P J L Dujon, c Fowler b Botham	8
M D Marshall, c Pringle b Willis	29
E A E Baptiste, c Downton b Willis	44
R A Harper, c Gatting b Botham	8
J Garner, c Downton b Botham	6
M A Small, not out	3
Extras (lb5, w1, nb7)	13
Total	245

Fall of wickets: 1-1, 2-18, 3-35, 4-138, 5-147, 6-173, 7-213, 8-231, 9-241
Bowling: Willis 19-5-48-2, Botham 27.4-6-103-8, Pringle 11-0-54-0, Foster 6-2-13-0, Miller 2-0-14-0

ENGLAND - Second Innings

G Fowler, lbw b Small	11
B C Broad, c Harper b Garner	0
D I Gower, c Lloyd b Small	21
A J Lamb, c Dujon b Marshall	110
M W Gatting, lbw b Marshall	29
I T Botham, lbw b Garner	81
P R Downton, lbw b Small	4
G Miller, b Harper	9
D R Pringle, lbw b Garner	8
N A Foster, not out	9
Extras (b4, lb7, w1, nb6)	18
Total (9 wkts)	300

Fall of wickets: 1-5, 2-33, 3-36, 4-88, 5-216, 6-230, 7-273, 8-290, 9-300
Bowling: Garner 30.3-3-91-3, Small 12-2-40-3, Marshall 22-6-85-2, Baptiste 26-8-48-0, Harper 8-1-18-1

WEST INDIES - Second Innings

C G Greenidge, not out	214
D L Haynes, run out	17
H A Gomes, not out	92
Extras (b4, lb4, nb13)	21
Total (1 wkt)	344

Fall of wickets: 1-57
Bowling: Willis 15-5-48-0, Botham 20-1-2-117-0, Pringle 8-0-44-0, Foster 12-0-45-0, Miller 11-0-45-0

West Indies won by 9 wickets

The message is clear. England were outclassed by a rampant West Indies

FINAL · SCORES

Headingley, Leeds, Third Test

ENGLAND - First Innings

G Fowler, lbw b Garner	10
B C Broad, c Lloyd b Harper	32
V P Terry, c Harper b Holding	8
D I Gower, lbw b Garner	2
A J Lamb, b Harper	100
I T Botham, c Dujon b Baptiste	45
P R Downton, c Lloyd b Harper	17
D R Pringle, c Haynes b Holding	19
P J W Allott, b Holding	3
N G B Cook, b Holding	1
R G D Willis, not out	4
Extras (b4, lb7, nb18)	29
Total	270

Fall of wickets: 1-13, 2-43, 3-53, 4-87, 5-172, 6-236, 7-237, 8-244, 9-254
Bowling: Garner 30-11-73-2, Marshall 6-4-6-0, Holding 29.2-8-70-4, Baptiste 13-1-45-1, Harper 19-6-47-3

WEST INDIES - First Innings

C G Greenidge, c Botham b Willis	10
D L Haynes, b Allott	18
H A Gomes, not out	104
I V A Richards, c Pringle b Allott	15
C H Lloyd, c Gower b Cook	48
P J L Dujon, lbw b Allott	26
E A E Baptiste, c Broad b Allott	0
R A Harper, c Downton b Allott	0
M A Holding, c Allott b Willis	59
J Garner, run out	0
M D Marshall, c Botham b Allott	4
Extras (lb3, nb15)	18
Total	302

Fall of wickets: 1-16, 2-43, 3-78, 4-148, 5-201, 6-206, 7-206, 8-288, 9-290
Bowling: Willis 18-1-123-2, Allott 26.5-7-71-6, Botham 7-0-45-0, Pringle 13-3-26-0, Cook 9-1-29-1

ENGLAND- Second Innings

G Fowler, c and b Marshall	50
B C Broad, c Baptiste b Marshall	2
V P Terry, lbw b Garner	1
D I Gower, c Dujon b Harper	43
A J Lamb, lbw b Marshall	3
I T Botham, c Dujon b Garner	14
P R Downton, c Dujon b Marshall	27
D R Pringle, lbw b Marshall	2
P J W Allott, lbw b Marshall	4
N G B Cook, c Lloyd b Marshall	0
R G D Willis, not out	5
Extras (lb6, nb2)	8
Total	159

Fall of wickets: 1-10, 2-13, 3-104, 4-106, 5-107, 6-135, 7-138, 8-140, 9-146
Bowling: Garner 16-7-37-2, Marshall 26-9-53-7, Holding 7-1-31-0, Harper 16-8-30-1

WEST INDIES - Second Innings

C G Greenidge, c Terry b Cook	49
D L Haynes, c Fowler b Cook	43
H A Gomes, not out	2
I V A Richards, not out	22
Extras (lb2, nb13)	15
Total (2 wkts)	131

Fall of wickets: 1-106, 2-108
Bowling: Willis 8-1-40-0, Allott 7-2-24-0, Pringle 8.3-2-25-0, Cook 9-2-27-2

West Indies won by 8 wickets

1986 St John's Recreation Ground

FIFTH TEST, 11-13, 15, 16 APRIL

Commentators: CHRISTOPHER MARTIN-JENKINS, HENRY BLOFELD, TONY COZIER
Summarisers: JACK BANNISTER, COLIN MILBURN

Captain David Gower relaxes on deck as England slip to defeat against the Windward Islands

After the humiliation of the 5-0 'blackwash' in 1984, David Gower led England in two series in which they very much restored their pride. In India, remarkably, they came back from losing the first Test to take the series and then the Ashes were regained in the summer with Gower himself leading from the front. He made three Test hundreds, one of them a double. As he held up a replica of the famous urn, Gower was even bold enough to say, 'Bring on the West Indies'. That winter he knew his side were bound for the Caribbean and the sternest test in international cricket. Quite probably, in true David Gower fashion, the tongue was in the cheek, but he had caught the euphoric mood of the moment with that bit of bravado.

Great as England's problems on the field seemed likely to be, there were to be quite a few off it. The first of these came with rumblings of disquiet over the presence in the party of a few players who had been to South Africa on the tour of 1982 and had incurred three-year bans. At the centre of this potential storm was the captain of that team, Graham Gooch, who was particularly unhappy about the writings on this subject of the Deputy Prime Minister of Antigua, Lester Bird. Antigua, as it happens, was to be the venue for the final Test of the series.

The relaxed, laissez-faire attitude of David Gower, which had carried him through India with its usual charm, was now proving an irritant to some onlookers.

This was the tour when Gower introduced optional net practice, and although the chances of beating the West Indies were one in a million, I think we should have made a more visible effort than we did.

There were also Ian Botham's problems with the newspaper stories.

HENRY BLOFELD

The press were fed an early gift when Gower was becalmed on a sailing trip round St Vincent as his side were going down to defeat at the hands of the Windward Islands. But there was a more serious on-the-field blow to come before the first Test.

In the One-Day International in Jamaica that immediately preceded the Test there, Mike Gatting was hit on the bridge of his nose as he attempted to hook Malcolm Marshall. It was badly broken and Gatting was soon on his way home for surgery on it. Gower had put his faith in Gatting the previous winter when, after his failures against the West Indies it had seemed his international career was over. Gatting had amply rewarded this vote of confidence, which had included being appointed vice-captain, so his departure now was a great loss.

The other crucial factor was the state of the pitch for that first Test in Kingston, which became a nightmare of inconsistent bounce, exploited to the full by the West Indian fast attack of Marshall, Garner, Patterson and Holding who bowled England out twice in the 150s, and shattered their nerve in the process. It led to a ten-wicket win for West Indies that was followed by similarly overwhelming victories in Trinidad, Barbados and Trinidad again. Viv Richards, in his first series against England as captain, was on the verge of being able to emulate his distinguished predecessor, Clive Lloyd, with a 5-0 thrashing of the old country. Where

Mike Gatting has his nose smashed by Malcolm Marshall in the one-day international in Jamaica. It was the moment England's mood changed

Test Match Special

better for Richards to achieve that feat than in his home island of Antigua in the final Test of the series?

The Recreation Ground at Antigua has a prison down one side, and the prisoners look after it. You can go out there and see the heavy roller being pushed by some chap doing life for murder and you had better make sure that your pocket handkerchief is still in your pocket when you get back to the pavilion!

When it was originally developed the money came from a Russian Jew, which was an odd sort of background for a cricket ground in the West Indies. It was also a noisy Test. The ground is very small and the PA announcer greeted every West Indian boundary and every England wicket with a burst of calypso music. We got to know the songs very well.

CHRISTOPHER MARTIN-JENKINS

On 11th April, Gower won the toss and put West Indies in to bat, partly to give his bowlers the best chance of an early breakthrough, but probably also defensively worrying about what the West Indian bowlers might do in any sort of helpful conditions. Ian Botham, Neil Foster and Richard Ellison were the trio of seam bowlers and it was Botham who took the first wicket, when he bowled Greenidge for 14. But Richie Richardson, another one in his home island, rather tucked into Botham.

HENRY BLOFELD *Here is Botham again, hair flopping, up. Bowls to Richardson and it's short. Richardson goes back, hits it over Robinson's head at cover, slashing, great slashing stroke and it goes away into the advertising signs over there on the east, the prison side of the ground for four runs. Well, it was short. It was only in his first over and he gave it everything, reminding me a little bit of a batsman called Colin Milburn.*
COLIN MILBURN *Well I don't know about that, second ball, but this is exactly how he played in Trinidad. He came in, particularly when poor Greg Thomas was bowling, and he just went for anything. Anything short, anything pitched up, he gave it the full works and that could very easily have gone straight down Tim Robinson's throat there at cover but unfortunately for England it went over his head for four.*
HENRY BLOFELD *Richardson's off the mark. He plays that way and in this series, by and large, has got away with it. Of course he played a marvellous innings, that 102 at Port-of-Spain in the second Test match. He really did very much set up West Indies' lead on that occasion. Botham in, bowls to Richardson who comes forward, drives it in the air past Gower there at mid-on. It was uppish, it fell just about parallel with Gower who chases it back, two-thirds of the way to the boundary, picks up this time in*

his right hand but doesn't throw because its. . . Richardson has just completed the second and they're not going to attempt a third. So 29 now for one. That was the inswinger. It was not quite a half-volley. He hit through the ball, through the line. It was uppish. It was to Gower's right but once again Richardson prepared to take Botham on. Botham won't be unhappy about that at all, I'm sure, because playing like this, Richardson is giving Botham a great chance of getting his 354th Test wicket. He's already got his 353rd this morning when he bowled Greenidge. Botham in, bowls now to Richardson. It's short. Richardson rather surprisingly didn't attempt to hook that. It was again coming into him but he just pulled away. It went past his waist through there, past his chest really, through to Paul Downton. And certainly the crowd have come awake with these two strokes of Richardson's, that slashing cut over cover's head and then the lofted on-drive. There's a great buzz going round the ground and, of course, second to Viv Richards of the present West Indian side, Richie Richardson is all Antigua's favourite son. Botham turns now. Richardson slender, waits for him, capless, hatless. Botham's in, bowls. He's forward driving, in the air over Botham's head and it's coming down to the pavilion rails here chased by Foster. He's not going to get it and it's four runs. Well, well, well. It was rather a good length ball, he came forward, hit through the line and hit it straight back over Botham's head for four. Desmond Haynes gives him a little round of applause. The crowd give him something more than that. The calypso band, I think it must be on a tape, is booming out and half the members of the stand to our left are doing the jump up which is of course the calypso dance. So, great merriment here in Antigua.

It was John Emburey who curbed this particular Antiguan celebration, turning the ball to have Richardson caught at bat-pad for 24. Emburey continued to cause problems and had Larry Gomes dropped at slip before he had scored, but he had to wait until Gomes had made 24 before he bowled him to make it 137 for three. Viv Richards started with five successive fours, but Botham continued to feed the hook shot and it paid off at last when Richards was caught by Gooch on the fine-leg boundary for 26. At 178 for 4, West Indies had certainly not broken free, though through the day Desmond Haynes had been heading steadily, despite giving three chances, towards a century. It was important to his side that he was still there at the end of the first day with 117 to his name. On the second day, Dujon went early, bowled by Foster for 21 and Haynes, even with five wickets down, was content to continue as sheet anchor, while Malcolm Marshall played the shots.

CHRISTOPHER MARTIN-JENKINS *Now Haynes, who's been patient as ever this morning, allowed himself few liberties, 127 not out facing Ellison as he comes in from the far end. Bowls a ball of half-volley length and it's whipped away off his toes by Haynes. The shot he plays so brilliantly. I think it is his shot really, a turn of the wrists and whipped away to square-leg. And that merits a calypso beat on the tape recording here. 281 for five and Marshall up to 29 and Haynes now to 131.*

Here comes Ellison, bowls again and that's mis-hooked, it's going to be caught at mid-on by Gatting and he is. So well done Ellison. His extra pace that he's worked up to in the last couple of hours paying him well there and Haynes, not quite in control of that hook shot, and his fine innings is over. It went fairly flat but at fairly comfortable height to Gatting at mid-on off the splice of the bat, and Desmond Haynes is out.

Wilf Slack gets as high as possible to keep the rising ball under control

With Haynes out for 131, Marshall continued to attack and a six over long-on brought up the 300. With Harper he added 70 for the seventh wicket before he was caught off Gooch for 60. In fact, the last four wickets were to bring the West Indies 193 runs, and Harper's eventual 73 turned a respectable total into something altogether more formidable, when they were all out for 474. But the fact that the tail had been able to score freely demonstrated that the pitch was a good one and by the close, England were 40 for no wicket.

Graham Gooch's opening partner in this Test was Wilf Slack, the St Vincent-born left-hander who had been brought out to West Indies from the England 'B' tour of Sri Lanka after Gatting's injury.

HENRY BLOFELD *97 for no wicket. Much England's best start of this series and, dare one say it, the West Indies are not used to not having success. They seem to expect it and, indeed, it has been theirs as of right against all countries in the last few years, but just at this moment they're being held up. Here is Patterson, in, bowls, and this time Slack goes back, a thick edge past third slip for four runs. Richardson just lopes back after it. It went away. It wasn't a catch. It went past Marshall, bouncing before it got within reach of the slips, went very quickly away and that is the hundred up, 101 for no wicket the score and perhaps not the best stroke of the morning to bring up that landmark, but nonetheless it was safe enough. 41 now to Slack. England's first century opening partnership of the series and how well these two have done.*

That was the best wicket of the series and they did finally produce some good batting.
CHRISTOPHER MARTIN-JENKINS

The opening pair put on 127 together, but that was followed by the sort of collapse which had become more familiar throughout that series from England. After Gooch had gone for 51 and Slack for 52, Robinson followed for 12 and Lamb for 1. It was 159 for four when Mike Gatting came out to play his first Test innings of the tour. He had returned from the surgery to his nose a month before and almost immediately had his thumb broken. His presence had been missed, but now he could only manage 15 before being caught behind off Garner, who also got Botham for 10 and Downton for 5 before the close of that second day. The saving grace for England was that their captain, David Gower was playing beautifully and was 70 not out at the end of the day when England were 263 for seven.

In the final session there was one unseemly incident when Viv Richards held the game up for ten minutes, protesting about the umpire's choice of a replacement ball.

Mike Gatting, having undergone surgery in England to his nose, returned to West Indies and had his thumb broken almost immediately. He played his first Test innings of the tour in Antigua

I think, perhaps, it showed to some extent the importance which Viv Richards attached to playing in Antigua and I rather think he would not have reacted as he did on any other ground. He behaved petulantly and arrogantly and stupidly which I think was out of character and he treated the umpires as if they were just a couple of naughty schoolboys instead of the two men who ought to have been in charge of the game. That was the one thing that Viv did wrong during the series and it was the series which saw the start of the acceptance of Richards as the right man to captain the West Indies.

CHRISTOPHER MARTIN-JENKINS

The first task for England on the fourth day was to reach the 275 runs they needed to avoid being asked to follow-on. The captain was the man to guide them to that.

CHRISTOPHER MARTIN-JENKINS *Two seventy-one for seven. Holding at full tilt goes running in again. Bowls to Gower. Short. Gower hooks him and there are the runs that save the follow-on. It's going up towards the mid-wicket boundary and Patterson can't catch it. The ball hits the little white fence and a cry of 'yes' from down below, from the England team who are very relieved that their captain has saved the follow on. He's taken his own score to 81 and England's total to two seventy-five for seven.*

The saving of the follow-on had surely given England the odds-on chance to draw this match. It would be nice for them now if Gower could go on to his hundred. Sadly for him and for the crowd who had appreciated his innings, he was caught behind off Marshall for 90, by which time he had already seen Marshall get Ellison for just 6 runs.

David Gower's 90 in Antigua was the nearest any Englishman got to scoring a century on that tour, which just underlined the foolishness of the England selectors in not taking him along in 1990.

He was England's most successful batsman by some way on this tour. He fought, like they all did, but they were not the first side to be simply outgunned and mown down by the West Indian fast bowlers.

HENRY BLOFELD

Foster and Emburey managed to take the score past 300 before Garner had Foster caught in the gully for 10. The West Indies had a lead of 164, to which they could start to add before lunch on the fourth day.

In the quest for quick runs they opened with Haynes and Richardson who obliged with a rapid hundred partnership before Emburey had Richardson caught for 31. If that first wicket stand was a good quick start for the West Indies, it was nothing compared to what was to come. Viv Richards had promoted himself to number three in the order and now he sauntered to the crease. His innings though, turned out to be anything but a saunter.

After ten balls he had made 24, which had included two sixes. In 46 minutes on that fourth afternoon he reached 50 off his 33rd ball — and that was the slowest part of his innings. The next 15 balls he received took him to 93 and he reached his hundred in a scarcely credible 56 balls and 81 minutes, a new world record.

Christopher Martin-Jenkins *In comes Emburey right arm over the wicket, bowls to Richards and he whips it away over to square-leg, going down towards Gooch and there is his hundred. Gooch, in fact, mis-fields and it goes for four and Richards waves his bat high the air, a broad grin on his face. The police come out to try to stop the spectators but they can't do so and one gentleman in a blue shirt tries to lift him off the ground. The police trying to protect the uncrowned king of Antigua at the end of what has been an absolutely brilliant hundred.*

It was a command performance after he had horrified the entire island by getting out to Botham for 26 in the first innings.

They could not believe it — everyone was scratching their heads — but he didn't half get it right in the second innings! He absolutely destroyed the bowling — Botham, Foster, Emburey and Ellison. It was pure strokeplay with very little slogging, although when Richards did slog, somehow it looked lovely.

HENRY BLOFELD

Test   Match   Special

Viv Richards cannot
contain his delight at
reaching his hundred
off only 56 balls. John
Emburey cannot believe
it, either

*T*here had been a suggestion in this series that Richards
was beginning to struggle to concentrate. When he
arrived at the crease in the second innings, it helped that
quick runs were clearly indicated. He knew exactly what
was required. He played with a carefree abandon that was
stunning to watch. The only innings I find remotely
comparable was Ian Botham's knock at Headingley in
1981. The circumstances were different, but the result was
the same. At one stage Botham, who needed two wickets to
overtake Lillee's world record for Test wickets, tried
containing Viv by packing the leg-side field and bowling a

tight leg-stump line. The first ball was swept for six and the second dispatched for six over extra cover. Richards was unstoppable.

CHRISTOPHER MARTIN-JENKINS

Richards capped his century with his seventh six before he declared, having made 110 not out from 58 balls in 83 minutes. The support he

David Gower's tenure as England captain was almost over, but the genius of his strokeplay was undiminished

had received from Haynes with 70 and Harper with 19 not out had paled into insignificance beside this prodigious performance which had set the Antigua Recreation Ground alight and, almost incidentally, given the West Indies the time to beat what must now surely have been a thoroughly demoralised England team. They had fifty minutes to bat on that fourth evening, time enough to lose two wickets. Slack was bowled by Garner for 8 and Robinson was run out for 3, but Gooch, importantly, was still there for the next day's battle. The only wicket to fall before lunch on that final day was that of the night-watchman, Richard Ellison, giving cause for some hope in England's heart that the match might be saved. But the pitch was now starting to make too many balls keep disconcertingly low. Gooch reached a lengthy defensive fifty but, at 51, after batting for 41 overs, he got one from Holding that nipped back to trap him leg-before. Gower then saw two other possible saviours of the game, Lamb and Gatting, quickly fall victim to the low bounce, both bowled for 1. It was 124 for six. For Botham, Richards shrewdly introduced the off-spinner, Harper, who Botham played onto his stumps for 13. Gower's three-hour innings of 21 at last ended at 166 for eight, when he edged Harper to Dujon. England did take the game six overs into the twenty of the last hour, but by then the result was not by then really in doubt. They were dismissed for 170 and the West Indies, with this 240 run win, had completed the second succesive whitewash, the margin of this victory owing so much to the incredible batting of the local hero Viv Richards.

If Richards was now secure as West Indies captain, David Gower's first spell as captain was almost over. He was to lead England in one more Test — a defeat by India at Lord's, before somewhat ironically giving way to the man whose Test career he had helped to salvage from ruin, Mike Gatting.

This was David Gower's tenth consecutive defeat as captain against the West Indies and, perhaps understandably, he seemed bankrupt of ideas. He never once lost his dignity under very trying circumstances and remained very popular with the West Indians, who love his batting. He did not quite have the drive to turn things round his way, but I think he was given an impossible mission. It was just a case that England might have lost three-nil rather than five-nil.

CHRISTOPHER MARTIN-JENKINS

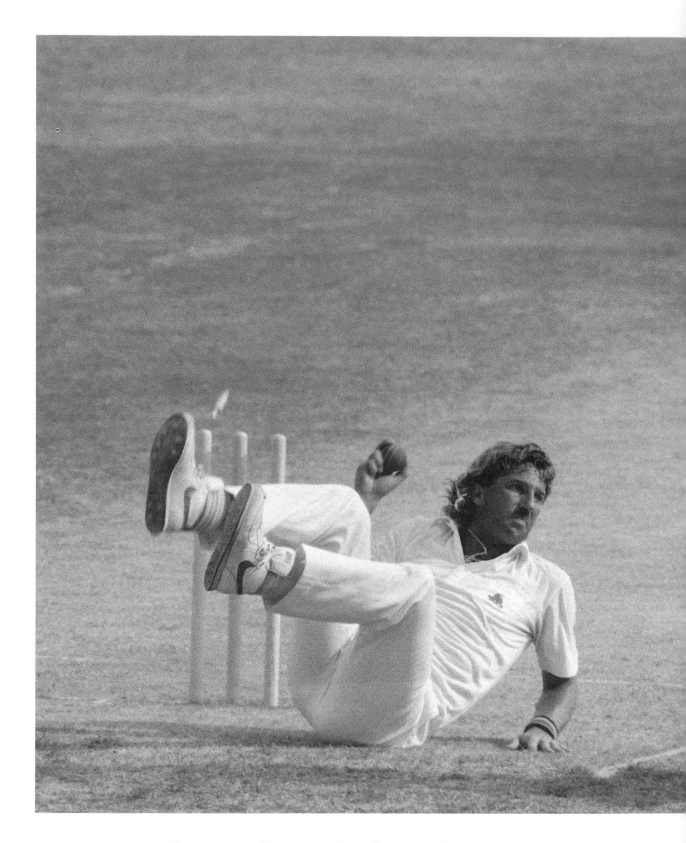

FINAL · SCORES

WEST INDIES - First Innings

C G Greenidge, b Botham	14
D L Haynes, c Gatting b Ellison	131
R B Richardson, c Slack b Emburey	24
H A Gomes, b Emburey	24
I V A Richards, c Gooch b Botham	26
P J L Dujon, b Foster	21
M D Marshall, c Gatting b Gooch	76
R A Harper, c Lamb b Foster	60
M A Holding, c Gower b Ellison	73
J Garner, run out	11
B P Patterson, not out	0
Extras (b2, lb11, w1)	14
Total	474

Fall of wickets: 1-23, 2-63, 3-137, 4-178, 5-232, 6-281, 7-351, 8-401, 9-450
Bowling: Botham 40-6-147-2, Foster 28-5-86-2, Ellison 24.3-3-114-2, Emburey 37-11-93-2, Gooch 5-2-21-1

ENGLAND - First Innings

G A Gooch, lbw b Holding	51
W N Slack, c Greenidge b Patterson	52
R T Robinson, b Marshall	12
D I Gower, c Dujon b Marshall	90
A J Lamb, c and b Harper	1
M W Gatting, c Dujon b Garner	15
I T Botham, c Harper b Garner	10
P R Downton, C Holding b Garner	5
R M Ellison, c Dujon b Marshall	0
J E Emburey, not out	7
N A Foster, c Holding b Garner	10
Extras (b5, lb6, nb40)	51
Total	310

Fall of wickets: 1-127, 2-132, 3-157, 4-159, 5-205, 6-213, 7-237, 8-289, 9-290
Bowling: Marshall 24-5-64-3, Garner 21.4-2-67-4, Patterson 14-2-49-1, Holding 20-3-71-1, Harper 26-7-45-1, Richards 2-0-3-0

WEST INDIES - Second Innings

D L Haynes, run out	70
R B Richardson, c Robinson b Emburey	31
I V A Richards, not out	110
R A Harper, not out	19
Extras (b4, lb9, w1, nb2)	16
Total (2 wkts)	246

Fall of wickets: 1-100, 2-161,
Bowling: Botham 15-0-78-0, Foster 10-0-40-0, Ellison 4-0-32-0, Emburey 14-0-83-1

ENGLAND - Second Innings

G A Gooch, lbw b Holding	51
W N Slack, b Garner	8
R T Robinson, run out	3
D I Gower, c Dujon b Harper	21
A J Lamb, b Marshall	1
M W Gatting, b Holding	1
I T Botham, b Harper	13
P R Downton, lbw b Marshall	13
R M Ellison, lbw b Garner	16
J E Emburey, c Richardson b Harper	0
N A Foster, not out	0
Extras (b10, lb10, w2, nb21)	43
Total	170

Fall of wickets: 1-14, 2-29, 3-84, 4-101, 5-112, 6-124, 7-147, 8-166, 9-168
Bowling: Marshall 16.1-6-25-2, Garner 17-5-38-2, Patterson 15-3-29-0, Holding 16-3-45-2, Harper 12-8-10-3, Richards 3-1-3-0

West Indies won by 240 runs

Ian Botham enjoys a rare success in Antigua, running out Desmond Haynes, for 70

1988 Headingley

FOURTH TEST, 21-23, 25, 26 JULY

Commentators: BRIAN JOHNSTON, DON MOSEY, TONY COZIER
Summarisers: FRED TRUEMAN, COLIN MILBURN

The issue of captaincy — normally an important topic in cricket — achieved much more prominence than usual in 1988. Mike Gatting had taken over from David Gower after the first Test of 1986 and, despite England's defeats that year at the hands of both India and New Zealand, he was the man to take the side to Australia that winter. There he not only successfully defended the Ashes, but carried off every trophy on offer. After that, the 1-0 series loss to Pakistan in 1987 — even though Pakistan had needed some rescuing weather early on — was very disappointing. So the World Cup campaign at the end of that year which ended with England's appearance in the final in Calcutta was perhaps a restoration of their reputation, even though Gatting's own rash reverse sweep contributed to the defeat in that final by Australia. It was followed immediately by a tour of Pakistan where local practices proved too sore a provocation to the straightforward Gatting's sense of

Shakoor Rana, the Pakistan umpire, Mike Gatting and England tour manager Peter Lush, the three figures at the centre of the row that led to the loss of a day's play in a Test match

fair play. In Faisalabad he was captured in close-up by the penetrating eyes of many different lenses in vitriolic exchange with umpire Shakoor Rana. He was not helped out of the limelight by the fact that England were doing rather well in the Test match at that stage. A day's play was lost and authority, as well as public opinion thousands of miles away, was outraged at the sight of the England captain involved in such an unseemly argument.

England had lost ten consecutive Test matches to the West Indies, so at the start of the summer of 1988 the first objective was to break that sequence with a draw at the very least. In the first Test at Trent Bridge, after England had had the encouragement of a clean sweep in the One-Day series, they got off to a fine start with a first wicket stand of 125 between Graham Gooch and Chris Broad. But Malcolm Marshall and a new name to English grounds, Curtly Ambrose, undid that good work with six and four wickets respectively. In reply to England's eventual 245, there were runs all the way down the order from West Indies in a total of 448 for nine declared. England had four sessions to survive and did so nobly, with Gooch making 146 and Gower 88 not out.

But during the course of that Nottingham Test other matters, linking the captain with a barmaid, had apparently been happening and they were brought to the attention of the public by a tabloid newspaper, ever alert to the needs of the nation. Gatting gave his explanation to the selectors, who said they believed him, and then promptly sacked him as captain anyway. It was hard to believe that the incident at Faisalablad had not had something to do with the outcome.

So England needed a new captain for the second Test at Lord's and they turned to Gatting's former vice-captain, John Emburey. He had a very encouraging start to his term of office as Graham Dilley put the West Indies in trouble on the first morning at 54 for five, and although they only got past 200

John Emburey took over from Mike Gatting to captain England at Lord's...

thanks to Logie and Dujon low in the order, the bowling of Marshall and a century in the second innings from Gordon Greenidge saw them to victory by 134 runs. At Old Trafford the West Indian bowlers shared the devastation of the first innings, but Marshall claimed the spoils for himself in the second with seven for 22 and a modest total was more than enough to beat England by an innings.

> *We didn't do very well and everything seemed to be going from bad to worse. It was really very depressing. They were just too good for us with this marvellous attack of Marshall and Ambrose.*
>
> BRIAN JOHNSTON

Test Match Special

There were two weeks before the fourth Test at Headingley and in that time the speculation raged about whether for that match, on a ground where a spinner in modern times was often not picked, John Emburey should be replaced as captain. Wider issues of pride, breaking away from the established group of professionals now so inured to failure and the forward planning of who would lead the side in India that winter were discussed in earnest.

Kent, with an apparently fairly average side, had made a very good start to the season and had been at the top of the Championship table

...then it was Chris Cowdrey's turn to take over the mantle of captaincy at Headingley

for a month. Their captain was Chris Cowdrey, son of Colin and, incidentally, godson of the Chairman of selectors, Peter May. His background for a return to something nearer the old amateur values of the game was impeccable. A likeable, busy all-rounder with the priceless ability to make things happen, he had played in all five Tests on the 1984/5 tour of India. With a run now in a series that England were unlikely to be able to save anyway, he might be just the man to take England back to India in the winter and restore much-needed pride. That was the course the selectors decided to follow eventually.

Cowdrey's two immediate predecessors to the captaincy were omitted: Emburey, because of the intention not to use a spinner and Gatting at his own request after returning unsuccessfully and dispiritedly at Old Trafford. Gatting's predecessor, David Gower, too, might well have lost his place, but this would be his hundredth Test and the new captain was not only a friend, but a great believer in his ability. The batting was shaken up, with Tim Curtis of Worcestershire coming in for his first cap to open with Gooch, Bill Athey returning for his first Test of the series and Robin Smith, tipped for some time as a future Test player, making his debut. Jack Richards, who had had some great moments on the last tour of Australia, replaced Paul Downton behind the stumps and Cowdrey's bowling would clearly be needed behind that of Dilley, Foster and Pringle.

If the context of the match with all that had led up to it were not bizarre enough, its start was a real collector's item, after the effects of an overnight deluge had been cleared for play to begin fifty minutes late.

Everything happens to dear old Dickie Bird. This time they had just started to play when suddenly the drains leaked up on to the ground and Dickie was dancing around with water up to his ankles.

BRIAN JOHNSTON

A blocked drain had created a morass at one end and play was held up for another two hours. When it did start again, Malcolm Marshall, who had already taken 26 wickets in the series, was soon in business.

DON MOSEY *Marshall away, turns, pitter patter of short steps, bowls and Gooch is beaten and he's out caught behind and he walks without waiting for a decision. England have lost their first wicket, Gooch caught Dujon bowled Marshall nine. England are 14 for one wicket.*

Tim Curtis' first Test innings ended at 12, when he was lbw trying to play Winston Benjamin through the on-side. His dismissal brought in David Gower with all England hoping he could celebrate his hundredth Test match in appropriate style.

DON MOSEY *Benjamin to Gower, and he plays and misses. . . Oh and he plays and edges and he's out! Caught! Oh dear, the little dab outside the off-stump. Gower departs again in his hundredth Test match out for 13 runs, caught Dujon, bowled Benjamin. And at tea which will now be taken, England are 58 for three.*
COLIN MILBURN *A disappointed David Gower there, I'm sure. The usual thing very casual outside the off-stump. It's a shame to see David play in this way at the moment, he's such a talented player, such a gifted player. I am sure in his early days he never played like that, never played so casual outside that off-stump.*

If the Yorkshire crowd had been denied a sparkling Gower innings to celebrate the occasion, they would certainly settle for runs from Bill

Athey who, despite his departure four years earlier to Gloucestershire, was still very much their man. Unfortunately, that too was not to be, as he was lbw to Ambrose for 16. At 80 for four, Allan Lamb was joined by Robin Smith and those two started to restore England's fortunes and even carry the attack to the West Indies. By the close they had put on 57 for the fifth wicket and the next day they played with even more freedom, taking their partnership into three figures as the West Indian bowlers began to show their frustration in an increasing number of bouncers. But it was not that which ended the stand.

TONY COZIER *Here is Ambrose, moves in now to bowl to Lamb, Lamb back and cuts it square on the off-side and they go for a quick single. Arthurton is out there fielding but he can't prevent the single as it goes to his left. So 183 for four, Smith 38, Lamb, with that single, 64.*

FRED TRUEMAN *Allan Lamb pulled a muscle I think. That's Allan Lamb — has he pulled a muscle running that quick single, Tony? That's what I was trying to point out to you, he certainly stopped halfway down the wicket and went into a very painful sort of limp.*

TONY COZIER *The physiotherapist is sprinting onto the field. Allan Lamb has taken off his right pad and is massaging the back of his right calf. Laurie Brown, the physiotherapist, is out there very quickly and it does look as if it isn't a pull, it may be a strain but he's down sitting down on the ground now, it may be cramp of course but I rather doubt it. And in fact it is Walsh who is signalling to the dressing room that Lamb who is on the turf getting attention, medical attention from the physiotherapist Laurie Brown, wants a runner. So the signal has gone to the dressing room. Right, so we'll see who emerges from the dressing room to run for Lamb who is really very, very affected by the injury. He can hardly stand up on it. Ooh, he's very ginger, in fact, on the right leg and he needs the support of the physiotherapist and he really is in quite a lot of distress, isn't he Fred?*

FRED TRUEMAN *Oh yes. As I say, I suddenly noticed, I watched to see if there was a quick single or possibly a run-out on or anything like that, which there wasn't, and he wasn't running to the danger end anyway, and suddenly I saw him pull up as though he'd been shot in the leg. It was not very nice at all and he's not walking as free as he would like to, and it will be interesting to see if a runner does come out, but he's certainly in some pain out there at the moment Tony, but we shall have to see. That will be a pity actually because I think the two lads were just starting to get a little bit on top of this West Indies bowling side, which suddenly for once in it's life, is not having everything its own way and its looking a little shattered.. They don't seem to know where their next wicket is coming from and they are not liking the fact.*

TONY COZIER *Yes, I think they have become accustomed to England rolling over and this is only the third century partnership of the series and* *at 183 for four, in fact, certainly there is no cause for panic in the West Indies camp, but the bowling hasn't been, and really wasn't yesterday either, the real quality it was in the first three Test matches. I suppose that with the experiences England have been suffering during this series and the previous two series, it is very heartening for them that a partnership has developed like this. In fact, we now can report that Allan Lamb is going off the field, he is going to retire hurt. He did strap the pad back on and he really is limping very badly as he hobbles off, being helped off by Laurie Brown the physiotherapist. And this is a crucial break and a crucial piece of bad luck for England to have a partnership really going having passed the century mark with Lamb leaving the partnership on 64, to have to retire hurt. And it brings the new England captain Chris Cowdrey into bat in his first Test match as captain in rather unusual circumstances.*

The muscle in Allan Lamb's right calf was torn and he was not able to bat again in that innings. His departure for 64 precipitated a collapse.

DON MOSEY *Ambrose taking up the attack from the football end, bowls to Smith who gets an extremely good one, there's an appeal and the whole of the West Indies side dance around and Dickie Bird, after taking a long time to make up his mind, says 'out'. So Smith goes caught Dujon bowled Ambrose for 38 and England are 183 for five.*

The question in everyone's minds now was: could the new England captain steady the boat?

DON MOSEY *Marshall from the Kirkstall Lane End bowls. I think this takes him on the pad outside the leg-stump. That runs away, but no stroke was offered and the crowd who were quick to applaud the England captain getting off the mark have to withdraw their applause so to speak. It was premature. Richards gives him a friendly pat on the back and no doubt muttered something about hard luck and 'don't worry it will come.' Marshall giving Cowdrey quite a testing time, bowls again and he's in front, lbw and trapped completely and there can be no doubt about that one. So poor Chris Cowdrey on his debut as the England captain lbw bowled Marshall no score and suddenly England, from being comfortable are in trouble at 183 for six.*

It was now Derek Pringle's turn to face a hostile Marshall in full flight and with the pressure on.

DON MOSEY *Richards at first slip, Hooper at second, Harper at third, Haynes in the gully and Logie at short-leg — they are the close catchers. The remainder of the field, at long-leg, cover point and mid-off and a mid-on. Marshall in, and that was a magnificent ball and he's out! It lifted,*

Test Match Special

brushed the glove I think and England are in serious trouble now at 185 for seven with Lamb also injured. Another splendid delivery from Marshall, another success for the West Indies, I think I'd better get out of this commentary seat before they're all out.

Meanwhile, the England wicket-keeper Jack Richards was preparing to face a new over from Ambrose.

BRIAN JOHNSTON *Away goes Ambrose now and bowls this one and Richards is clean bowled. He pushed forward for that one and he is clean bowled. The bails are off, Richards walks back clean bowled by Ambrose and one really does not know what to say. This is a sensational collapse when you consider the wickets have fallen like ninepins as soon as Lamb went off injured. So it's really a very sad morning for England. That means Ambrose has now taken three wickets for 52.*

Last-man Graham Dilley saw England past the 200 before facing up to Ambrose again.

TONY COZIER *Ambrose to Dilley and Dilley swings at it. He's out, caught, the end of the innings, Hooper takes the catch at second slip. So Dilley has gone caught by Hooper off Harper for eight, England are all out 201. Allan Lamb who retired hurt is so badly hurt in fact that he is unable to continue his innings. At the end of the innings Dilley has gone, caught by Hooper bowled Ambrose for eight and the England innings comes to a swift end with quite a dramatic collapse once Allan Lamb had retired hurt.*

The West Indies had been having their own injury problems prior to this Test match. Neither Greenidge nor Richardson, who had opened in the previous Test, was available for this one, but Desmond Haynes, who had missed Old Trafford, was back with a new opening partner, Jeffrey Dujon, who had been having such a good series with the bat. Dujon started well, making 13 of the first 15 runs, before he was caught at cover off Dilley. Carl Hooper made 19 before he was lbw to Foster. At 61 for two in came Viv Richards and very soon started to look in ominously good form.

TONY COZIER *Here is Richards driving down to Dilley, straight through Dilley for four runs, a big drive by Richards but straight through Dilley and it went straight through him to the boundary for four. In fact that was a bad bit of fielding, it seemed to me as if Dilley was sleeping and when the ball came to him he was very late getting there.*
FRED TRUEMAN *If he was asleep Tony, the way he hit that ball, I tell you what it wouldn't half have woken him up, because he didn't half give it a belt, oh dear what a beautiful shot. I mean he hit it with awesome power*

didn't he, dear, dear, dear. It's a wonder Dilley wasn't hung on to it when it was going through the fence. He did hit it hard.

TONY COZIER *So 97 for two, as Foster is in to Richards who pulls it, beautifully caught by Curtis at square-leg. Magnificent catch. Richards pulling low and hard and Curtis throwing himself to his right making a superb diving catch in front of the umpire. Richards caught Curtis bowled Foster 18, the West Indies 97 for three.*

FRED TRUEMAN *Well what wonderful cricket we've just seen there in three minutes. We saw a majestic shot through the off-side, through extra cover which was far too hot for Dilley to stop, in fact Dilley is still holding his hand where that ball went through him, and then we saw not a good delivery from Foster, a short one, a magnificent hook shot by Richards, but what a marvellous catch by Curtis, flinging himself to his right to a very low ball travelling very fast and hanging on to it both hands. It was really a marvellous piece of cricket to watch, the sort of cricket that crowds love to see, and that is a catch that Viv Richards won't forget in a hurry and Tim Curtis will remember for the rest of his life. It was a magnificent catch.*

After the departure of Richards for 18, Gus Logie joined Haynes in a stand of 40 for the fourth wicket which saw Haynes to a painstaking fifty. He was out lbw to Derek Pringle in the fortieth over of the innings for 54. Pringle also had Logie caught at mid-on for a much more rapid 44 and at the end of the second day the West Indies were 45 runs behind at 156 for five.

Saturday — always a great occasion at Headingley — was ruined by rain, which allowed less than two hours' play. In that time the West Indies took the lead and lost three more wickets, so that at the close of the third day they stood 37 runs ahead at 238 for seven. The time lost could well be crucial to England in saving the match.

With Harper still there over the rest day, there were more runs for West Indies on the Monday morning. Harper himself took his score to 56 in an eventual total of 275 — a lead of 74. It was a good performance by the England bowlers, but what Pringle with five wickets and Foster with three could do, the hostile West Indian pace quartet was liable to do even better.

Nonetheless, Gooch and Curtis started well, putting on 56, before Curtis was beaten for sheer pace and bowled by Ambrose for 12. Gooch and Athey saw England into credit, before Gooch was caught at second slip for 50 off Walsh. David Gower's first innings 13 had taken him to 6,998 runs in Test cricket. Coming in now he was able to take that tally to a nice round seven thousand. In Saturday's rain he had spent some time in the Test Match Special box. Brian Johnston had suggested to him that 'laid back' were two words he must be sick of hearing in conjunction with his name. 'No', Gower replied. 'The two words I'm most fed up with hearing are 'caught Dujon'.' It was prophetic.

Test Match Special

Tim Curtis is beaten for pace by Curtly Ambrose during the second innings

DON MOSEY *Marshall, slowly back to his mark, taking his time about this but there's nothing slow about his approach to the wicket as it begins now, bowls to Gower, who attempts to swing it down the leg-side and he's out caught by Dujon. That's the way he used to get out regularly before slip catches took over. Fine catch by Dujon but David Gower having just completed 7,000 runs in Test cricket departs, caught Dujon bowled Marshall for two. England are 85 for three and now in a spot of trouble.*

As Gower departed for the pavilion in dejection that his hundredth Test should be memorable for all the wrong reasons, there was the inescapable feeling that he would not play in another Test that summer

Test Match Special

— and so it proved. On this occasion his wicket had come in the early stages of yet another collapse.

TONY COZIER *At the moment here is Walsh, comes in now to Athey and beats him outside the off-stump and he's caught behind. Walsh beats Athey outside the off-stump, finds the edge, Dujon takes the catch, England are really struggling now. They are 85 for four with Athey caught Dujon, bowled by Walsh for 11.*

Allan Lamb and Robin Smith dragged England past the 100 mark and then came another over from Marshall.

DON MOSEY *There goes Marshall, bowls to Smith, who's rapped on the pad, there's an appeal and he's out Smith lbw, bowled Marshall 11, England now in deepest trouble at 105 for five.*

After his first innings duck, the England captain Chris Cowdrey was hoping for better fortune this time round.

DON MOSEY *Here's Walsh bowling to Cowdrey, who's bowled! Beaten for pace off the pitch, late on it and the middle-stump sagged drunkenly backwards, the West Indians leap in jubilation. The old baseball players' handshake is being freely exchanged all round, and as Fred Trueman was forecasting a moment ago, this could be all over tonight. England are 105 for six and bear in mind that Allan Lamb should really not be allowed to bat because of a torn calf muscle and I don't think the selectors will allow him to come out and bat. Yes he's coming out now with a runner, well I would have thought they would have saved him right to the end just to see what happens, see if there was any point in it, but if he damages that calf muscle any more it could have a very serious effect on his career. Nevertheless, a very gallant gesture that is being warmly applauded by the crowd as he comes out.*

Like their captain, Jack Richards and Derek Pringle were both clean bowled by pace. In their case by Ambrose and Benjamin. Then Foster went, caught at second slip, to give Benjamin his second wicket for no runs at that stage. The hobbling Lamb was left only with Graham Dilley for company.

TONY COZIER *England 138 for nine as Ambrose is on the way to Lamb, Lamb drives towards mid-off and then hobbles on one leg, the left leg, the right leg which has this torn calf muscle cocked up behind him and hobbling across the pitch there. Really has had to endure a lot has Allan Lamb.*
COLIN MILBURN *I wonder if he's had an injection. I haven't heard, but I*

Jeffrey Dujon was promoted to open the West Indies batting in place of Greenidge, who was injured. Here, he is rocked back by a nasty delivery from Graham Dilley, with wicket-keeper Jack Richards looking interested

presume he must have done to kill the pain. Here is Ambrose, comes in, bright sunshine now as he's on the way. Lamb flashes outside the off-stump, that's the end of the innings, Ambrose gets the wicket. England all out for 138, Lamb caught Dujon bowled by Ambrose for 19. A long and extremely courageous innings by Lamb lasting for 89 minutes, 59 deliveries, finally caught by Dujon off Ambrose. England all out 138 in their second innings which means that West Indies will have 65 runs to win the match.

Allan Lamb's courageous innings had at least spared England the humiliation of a four-day defeat, but there was no redemption from the weather and acknowledging defeat, the England captain put himself on for the eighth over of the final morning.

Test Match Special

TONY COZIER *The West Indies are within two of victory. They are 63
without loss, Haynes has got 25, Dujon has got 36 and it will be Dujon
who will face the new England captain Chris Cowdrey with two runs
required. Dujon flicks it away and that's the winning hit, flicked it away
down behind square and it will go for four. Dujon finishes with 40, the
West Indies 67 without loss have won the fourth Cornhill Test by ten
wickets, they take the series 3-0 and retain the Wisden Trophy.*

With that ten-wicket victory the West Indies had secured
another series win over England. Only one Test remained. Chris
Cowdrey, in his original appointment had been given the
captaincy for that match at the Oval, too. However, in the
intervening few days, he was hit on the foot in a county match
and declared himself doubtful to selectors who, he later felt,
were not too anxious for him to recover his fitness. Instead,
they turned to their fourth captain of the season, Graham Gooch. He
could not inspire an England victory there, but there was a feeling that
some pride had returned in Foster's five first innings wickets which gave
England a first innings lead and the new captain's second innings 84,
though no one else could stay with him, and the West Indies enjoyed an
eight-wicket win.

**Former England captain
Mike Gatting joins
Graham Gooch and
Micky Stewart on the
balcony during
the match**

There was to be one more Test match that summer, in which
Graham Gooch ended the dismal England record of 18 games without a
win by defeating Sri Lanka at Lord's. In disillusionment, Chris Cowdrey
was fined by the Test and County Cricket Board for voicing his feelings
in a newspaper article and eventually he was to join Mike Gatting's team
in South Africa in early 1990.

Test   Match   Special

Test Match Special

FINAL · SCORES

ENGLAND - First Innings

G A Gooch, c Dujon b Marshall	9
T S Curtis, lbw b Benjamin	12
C W J Athey, lbw b Ambrose	16
D I Gower, c Dujon b Benjamin	13
A J Lamb, retired hurt	64
R A Smith, c Dujon b Ambrose	38
C S Cowdrey, lbw b Marshall	0
C J Richards, b Ambrose	2
D R Pringle, c Dujon b Marshall	0
N A Foster, not out	8
G R Dilley, c Hooper b Ambrose	8
Extras (b1, lb18, w6, nb6)	31
Total	201

Fall of wickets: 1-14, 2-43, 3-58, 4-80, 5-183, 6-183, 7-185, 8-185, 9-201
Bowling: Marshall 23-8-55-3, Ambrose 25.1-8-58-4, Benjamin 9-2-27-2, Walsh 12-4-42-0

WEST INDIES - First Innings

D L Haynes, lbw b Pringle	54
P J L Dujon, c Smith b Dilley	13
C L Hooper, lbw b Foster	19
I V A Richards, c Curtis b Foster	18
A L Logie, c Foster b Pringle	44
K L T Arthurton, c Richards b Pringle	27
R A Harper, c Gower b Foster	56
M D Marshall, c Gooch b Pringle	3
C E L Ambrose, lbw b Pringle	8
W K M Benjamin, run out	9
C A Walsh, not out	9
Extras (lb15)	15
Total	275

Fall of wickets: 1-15, 2-61, 3-97, 4-137, 5-156, 6-194, 7-210, 8-222, 9-245, 10-275
Bowling: Dilley 20-5-59-1, Foster 32.2-6-98-3, Pringle 27-7-95-5, Cowdrey 2-0-8-0

ENGLAND - Second Innings

G A Gooch, c Hooper b Walsh	50
T S Curtis, b Ambrose	12
C W J Athey, c Dujon b Walsh	11
D I Gower, c Dujon b Marshall	2
A J Lamb, c Dujon b Ambrose	19
R A Smith, lbw b Marshall	11
C S Cowdrey, b Walsh	5
C J Richards, b Ambrose	8
D R Pringle, b Benjamin	3
N A Foster, c Hooper b Benjamin	0
G R Dilley, not out	2
Extras (b3, lb8, nb4)	15
Total	138

Fall of wickets: 1-56, 2-80, 3-85, 4-85, 5-105, 6-105, 7-127, 8-132, 9-132, 10-138
Bowling: Marshall 17-4-47-2, Ambrose 19.5-4-40-3, Benjamin 5-4-2-2, Walsh 20-9-38-3

WEST INDIES - Second Innings

D L Haynes, not out	25
P J L Dujon, not out	40
Extras (lb2)	2
Total (0 wkt)	67

Bowling: Dilley 4-0-16-0, Foster 7-1-36-0, Cowdrey 3.3-0-13-0

West Indies won by 10 wickets

Unbearable moments at Headingley for three England captains of past and present

Test Match Special

1990 Sabina Park and Queen's Park Oval

FIRST TEST, 24-26 FEBRUARY, 1 MARCH
THIRD TEST, 23-25, 27, 28 MARCH

Commentators: TONY COZIER, REDS PEREIRA,
CHRISTOPHER MARTIN-JENKINS, ANDREW MASON
Summarisers: DAVID GOWER, MICHAEL HOLDING, MAURICE FOSTER,
TREVOR BAILEY, GERRY GOMEZ, DERYCK MURRAY

In the English summer of 1989, England were the victims of a smash-and-grab raid on the Ashes by Australia. If the 4-0 defeat was a major disappointment to the re-appointed England captain, David Gower, it presented fundamental batting problems for Graham Gooch, who asked to be excluded from the fifth Test. As the end of the season approached, the speculation about who would lead England in the Caribbean in the new year was rife. The field was slightly trimmed by the announcement in London of another unofficial tour of South Africa which included three of the four England captains of 1988: Mike Gatting, John Emburey and Chris Cowdrey.

The mantle fell on the shoulders of Graham Gooch and, perhaps more surprising than that, his predecessor, David Gower, was omitted from the touring team. A new regime of physical fitness was declared, helped by the fact that departure for the West Indies was not until the end of January. The captain himself, who had been so unhappy on his previous tour there, had a single-minded determination about his approach. The first two one-day internationals saw England, to the surprise of many onlookers, play themselves into good positions before each was washed out by rain. But West Indians had seen nothing to cause them any concern. They were simply the best team in the world, with an awesome bowling attack and a settled batting line-up full of potential match-winners.

The build-up to the first Test in Jamaica included a large dinner to mark the fortieth anniversary of West Indies' first win in England. The assembly of famous names served to heighten the anticipation of the match and there was much recalling of the last Test against England on this ground when, on a dangerously uneven pitch, England's batsmen had been happy enough to escape with their lives. The pitch this time was not apparently of such dubious quality, but no dispassionate onlooker had any real doubt about the result.

West Indies captain Viv Richards was looking forward to another tussle with the auld enemy

The West Indies certainly underestimated the opposition. There was complacency. They seemed to feel that all they had to do was turn up to win the match, not perhaps realising that England had come extremely well prepared and were a different team psychologically, if not in talent. The two leading West Indian players came into the match underprepared. Viv Richards had played in only two first class matches in the Red Stripe Cup which preceded the Test match and he had done nothing really, because of a broken finger which he had sustained in the first of those games. Malcolm Marshall, through a series of injuries, had also been limited to two Red Stripe matches.

TONY COZIER

England decided to ape the West Indies with an attack based on seam bowling when they left out the spinner on the morning of the match. Viv Richards won the toss and his experienced opening pair of Gordon Greenidge and Desmond Haynes gave the West Indies a start that suggested nothing of any trouble to come. They were starting to think about lunch when Greenidge turned one down to deep fine-leg where the fielder was the Jamaican-born Devon Malcolm. Greenidge would have known that Malcolm was not the best fielder in the England side and, sure enough, he fumbled, so Greenidge called for the second run. What he seemed to have forgotten was that Malcolm had an excellent, powerful throwing arm and he found himself run out for 32. Still, 72 for one at lunch represented a fair morning's work.

After lunch Gooch brought David Capel on and in his third over Richie Richardson hooked at him and was caught at square-leg off the top edge. Four overs later Capel also had Carlisle Best caught behind and in the following over Gladstone Small held on to a hard return catch to

England team-mates congratulate Gladstone Small on taking the vital wicket of Desmond Haynes

remove Haynes for 36. It was 92 for four, but there was still some useful batting to come. A quarter of an hour before tea, though, there was a whiff of danger when Richards pulled at Malcolm and was lbw for 21. To claim the West Indian captain as his first Test victim in his native island was a great moment for the big Derbyshire pace bowler.

The final session of that first day belonged to Angus Fraser. With the first ball after tea he had Carl Hooper caught at mid-wicket for 20 and in the same over bowled Malcolm Marshall for a duck. In six overs after that interval, in fact, he took five for 6 and the West Indies had lost their last five wickets for 20 runs to be all out for 164.

There were nominally 24 overs still to go on the first day when England started their reply. In the event, although play went forty minutes into overtime — as was to be normal practice in this series — only 18 of those overs were bowled, in which time England made 80, though they lost Gooch caught down the leg side for 18 and Alec Stewart in his first Test caught at slip as he tried to avoid a bouncer from Ian Bishop for 13. Despite those losses it had been quite an encouraging start for England.

As controversial as the omission of David Gower from the touring team had been the inclusion of Wayne Larkins of Northamptonshire as the only other opening batsman apart from Gooch. Now he showed the doubters why the selectors and particularly the captain had recalled him to the colours at the age of 36. For the first hour and a half of the second day he and Allan Lamb set about consolidating their promising position with a third wicket stand of 56, which ended when Larkins got one from Walsh that kept low to have him lbw for 46. At 116 for three, England were now only 48 behind.

The best was yet to come as Lamb was joined now by Robin Smith. Through the afternoon, riding the luck of Lamb being dropped behind the wicket on 30, they relentlessly piled up the runs and less than half way through that session two fours from Lamb saw them into the lead. Tea was taken with England already 59 runs ahead, and afterwards the South African born pair continued to amass these unexpected riches.

Angus Fraser claims another wicket in his first-innings haul of five for 28 in the Jamaica Test

REDS PEREIRA *In comes Best, that's tossed up and again we see this ball eluding Richards. On that occasion it was to the right and he got a bit of a bad bounce there, went down and the ball just hopped up, beat him to the right hand and that's 50 for Smith. Acknowledging the applause and I think that the purists here even if they've come to support the West Indies, applauding that this young man has battled away and played with a lot of dedication and technique and skill.*

MICHAEL HOLDING *A very good 50 from Robin Smith. Many people in England would have seen Robin Smith make quite a lot of runs. This is not very unusual for him but what is unusual is the length of time that he has taken to make this 50. Robin Smith is known to be quite an attacking player especially off the back foot, cuts and pulls strongly, very hard through the off-side and the on-side, but he has tempered his aggression in this innings because he knows that England need the type of innings that he's playing at the moment. Slow, dedicated innings, waiting for the bad ball, pushing around getting singles, twos and despatching the bad balls whenever they appear. England are in no hurry at all. They have got two hundred runs on the board a lead of what, 83 runs over the West Indies first innings so far and going along merrily.*

Test Match Special

I remember talking to Robin Smith in the bar after his painstaking but vital 57 in the first innings. Robin said he could not remember a single shot that had given him satisfaction but I fancy in years to come he will remember the innings itself with great satisfaction.

CHRISTOPHER MARTIN-JENKINS

ANDREW MASON *Here's Bishop on the way from the far end to bowl to Allan Lamb who's on 99. He comes up now, goes past the umpire, bowls to Lamb and Lamb gets a ball . . . swung away. Four runs, that's his hundred! Oh what a way to get a hundred too! And he punches the air in triumph. A short ball and Lamb just helped it down behind square for four. He comes down now, takes the helmet off, his bat is raised and the whole England team applauding the work of Allan Lamb. Sabina Park happy with the work of Lamb. He batted beautifully, it was a short ball and he hit it down to backward square for four. So Lamb 103 and England marching on, 257 for three.*

Marshall did not bowl much and, his shortage of cricket showed. Lamb made the comment that he threw in the towel.

TONY COZIER

Twelfth-man Chris Lewis provides liquid refreshments for Lamb and Smith during their 172-run partnership

Jamaica had rested Patterson, Walsh and Dujon from the preceding match and they looked a little rusty coming into the Test arena. Dujon dropped Lamb at a vital stage and neither Walsh nor Patterson bowled especially well.

CHRISTOPHER MARTIN-JENKINS

Test Match Special

A typical Allan Lamb pull shot for four as the South African born batsman approaches yet another century for England against West Indies

Lamb's century had been his first outside England and he had had to sweat on 99 twice, because of a scoreboard error which gave him two opportunities to celebrate getting to three figures. This fourth wicket partnership added 172 in just over three and a half hours, not only taking England past the West Indies' total, but over a hundred runs into the lead.

CHRISTOPHER MARTIN-JENKINS *And both Lamb and Smith there clearly feeling the heat now, bent over and just taking a breather and running threes on an afternoon like that when you've been batting for as long as these two have is quite an exhausting business. But if they're tired imagine what the bowlers must be feeling because they've just had one success to lighten the spirit. Two eighty-eight for three. The sun beginning to get just a bit lower, the shadows lengthen almost to the same size as the men who are throwing them. As Bishop bowls on the off-stump. He's caught. Smith caught at second slip by Best as he carved at that ball off the back foot and Best this electrically quick slip fielder got both hands to it and took it beautifully and threw the ball up in the air. So this long and noble stand between the two South African-born English batsmen, Allan Lamb and Robin Smith, ends with Smith caught by Best off Bishop for 57, and England have lost their fourth wicket at 288.*

England's joy at having tamed the West Indies attack to this extent could not entirely be dampened by the loss of five wickets in the last hour-and-a-half of play, which was only halted after 55 minutes of overtime because of the slow over-rate. Even then there were seven overs unbowled. One of those five men out was Allan Lamb, after six magnificent hours' batting.

TONY COZIER *So Lamb who had a little period about 20 minutes ago, 15 minutes ago where he seemed to be suffering from tiredness. He played a number of loose shots. Now Walsh comes in to bowl to him and he's edged it. He's out, caught at first slip by Hooper. Lamb caught Hooper, bowled Walsh 132. England 315 for six and we'll have two new batsmen neither of whom have scored. So Allan Lamb after a superb century, his tenth in Test cricket, goes back to a standing ovation from the George Headley stand and he deserves it. Caught Hooper bowled Walsh, 132. Viv Richards also joins the applause out there as do many of the other West Indians and it will be little Jack Russell, the wicket-keeper, who will come in to replace him. England 315 for six with Lamb, caught Hooper bowled Walsh, 132.*
DAVID GOWER *That was a marvellous innings from Allan Lamb. Certainly worth a bottle of Bollinger if he can find one in Kingston tonight*

T e s t   M a t c h   S p e c i a l

to help him celebrate. At the end of the innings there Courtney Walsh still plugging away as we'd just been talking about. In his 20th over of the day, got one on the right line just outside off-stump, to bounce, to do a little bit more, just to go away a fraction from Allan Lamb and again well taken by the only slip that was posted there by Viv Richards.

Starting the third day at 342 for eight, England's last two wickets managed to add another 22 runs before Courtney Walsh ended the innings in two balls to give himself five wickets and England a lead of exactly 200.

Devon Malcolm, in his native Jamaica, was keen to give the locals a performance to remember him by. He had just been out first ball, but his one wicket had been that of Viv Richards in the first innings and he had been responsible for that crucial run out of Gordon Greenidge. He was to have more to enjoy in the second innings.

MAURICE FOSTER *I think Graham Gooch must be very happy at the moment. It's, it's nice to have a lead of 200 where he can afford to attack for a long time. One would feel that Gooch would be able to attack up to about 70-80 runs or so before probably getting a little bit defensive but not over-defensive mind you, because he's looking to bowl out the West Indies.*
ANDREW MASON *Now Malcolm comes up once more to bowl to Haynes who goes to 14. He's up to the wicket now and bowls to Haynes. Haynes gets a ball pitched up. He's bowled him, leg-stump! Desmond Haynes coming too far across the line, his leg-stump is out of the ground. It was a full toss. He came inside the line looking to whip the ball on the on-side and Malcolm strikes an important blow, Haynes bowled for 14.*

Gordon Greenidge and Richie Richardson started to bring the West Indies back into the reckoning with a second wicket stand of 43. Richardson tantalisingly survived a chance between wicket-keeper and first slip early on, but at last Fraser had him lbw, trying to turn a ball to leg for 25. Five overs later it was Malcolm who struck again, having Greenidge caught at cover point off an edged drive for 36. From 87 for three, Carlisle Best and Carl Hooper brought the hundred up, but at 112 Gladstone Small got Hooper's wicket from a juggled catch in the slips. That brought together Best and Richards in a stand which started to blossom and cause some anxiety in English hearts as, with only four wickets down, they began to threaten England's lead.

CHRISTOPHER MARTIN-JENKINS *Here comes Capel and bowls again to Richards who goes forward and that's the famous Richards shot hit through mid-wicket, just leaning into the ball and working it away in to the gap at mid-wicket. Perfectly respectable ball really, possibly a fraction over-pitched, but taken from perhaps middle-stump, perhaps even middle and off,*

A short delivery is stylishly despatched to the boundary by West Indies opener, Gordon Greenidge

Test Match Special

but that massive physique going across and just working the ball away as simply as you like into the mid-wicket gap. So one feels just at the moment that the initiative is starting to switch towards the batsmen. Still they've got to be aware of any over confidence, but it is looking comfortable at the moment. One-sixty-five for four and Richards moves to 28. Two fours in this over.

The fifty partnership had been posted and both batsmen looked well set for big scores.

TONY COZIER *Best has got 48 and faces Malcolm now as Best flicks it through the on-side. That will be his 50. His first 50 in Test cricket as they come for the second run. Hussain is after it from backward square-leg and Carlisle Best gets his 50, an immensely popular cricketer here in Jamaica where he's scored so many runs. Raising his bat, priceless innings from Best. So he's got a half century. Richards comes down the wicket to have a word with him and Carlisle Best's 50 in his fourth Test match.*

Malcolm was nearing the end of his spell but Gooch decided to persist with his main strike bowler.

TONY COZIER *So Malcolm, two very good wickets, he took care of the two opening batsmen. In he comes now to bowl to Richards. Richards 33 and Richards goes back and bangs it through the covers for four. Short ball, outside the off-stump and Richards getting up to his full height and banging it away down between cover point and extra cover for four. Richards on to 37 and the West Indies now move up to 192 for four, just eight runs now needed to erase the deficit. Starting to get back into contention here, the West Indies. A big deficit still. England in the ascendancy, but with Richards now looking better and better with every stroke and Carlisle Best in determined form, a partnership between the two of them already worth 80 for the fifth wicket. Gooch sends his cover back on the boundary. Smith has gone right back in to the sweeper position under the stand of the South Camp Road side on the eastern side of the ground, as Malcolm now is on the way again to Richards and Richards is bowled, played right over the top of it. A yorker-length ball as Richards played around it, the leg-stump has been knocked back. England are absolutely jubilant. Devon Malcolm has struck an absolutely decisive blow by bowling the dangerous Vivian Richards for 37.*
Here's Malcolm. Drive by Dujon, lovely shot down through extra cover for four. What a way to get off the mark and what a way to send the West Indies into the lead. They've gone past the 200. They're now 202 for five and the glorious, typically elegant extra cover drive by Jeffrey Dujon, left leg right out to the ball, beautiful flourish of the bat and through extra cover for four to get off the mark. West Indies 202 for five now. 56 to the

non-striker, Best. Richards the last man out. Bowled in the previous over from Malcolm for 37 as Malcolm, from the Northern end, now to Dujon and Dujon goes back and forces it through extra cover. That's a glorious shot once more. That's four runs. That is a magnificent shot from Dujon in absolute contrast to the previous one, even though in the same area, down through extra cover. This one was short outside the off-stump. He went off the back foot this time and with a full flourish of the bat hit it through extra cover for four. The previous one was well up to him, he came forward. This one he went back. Both the same effect, two boundaries. He's eight. It's 206 for five and Jeffrey Dujon has brought Sabina Park to life.

Sixteen runs later and Glandstone Small came into the action at a most crucial stage.

ANDREW MASON *It's going to be Small to bowl to Best who's on 64. He comes up now and bowls to Best and Best is forward. He's caught, yes he is at the second slip position, ball outside the off-stump, Best pushed at it, the outside edge found and Gooch holding on to the catch and Small strikes an important blow with the West Indies now 222 for the loss of six. Carlisle Best after batting for a long time getting a ball outside the off-stump. He pushed rather tentatively at it, the outside edge found Gooch at second slip delighted to come up with the catch. Carlisle Best goes for 64 now with the West Indies 222 for the loss of six. In reality 22 runs on for six wickets and the applause you can pick up in the background is for Carlisle Alonsa Best who stayed around for a long time but I have a strong feeling, not long enough.*

DAVID GOWER *Carlisle Best, after a long, long stay at the crease has finally gone. We were talking just a moment ago about perhaps there are one or two failures of concentration by Carlisle Best there and finally Gladstone Small is rewarded yet again for his persistence outside the off-stump. Another very good ball. The right, absolutely the right sort of line. He drew Best into the shot. Best could only steer it to second slip where Graham Gooch was delighted to take the catch and now, at 222 for six, double Nelson striking, the West Indies have got a lot of pressure on them.*

ANDREW MASON *Here is Malcolm, up and bowls to Dujon and Dujon is bowled. Dujon is bowled middle-stump The ball cut back at him. In fact the middle-stump is completely out of the ground. Jeffrey Dujon is bowled by Malcolm to a ball that cut back at him, perhaps there was a little bit of inside edge there. Dujon looked completely surprised but Malcolm strikes and strikes another important blow. The West Indies further in the mire now at seven for 222 and double Nelson striking once again.*

There was one more wicket on that third evening, to send the West Indies into the rest day at 229 for eight with a lead of only 29 runs. On both sides of the Atlantic the situation took quite a bit of believing.

If you had shown the scores to someone who did not know what had gone on and not given him the teams against those scores, he would have put the teams the wrong way round. They were very similar to scores we had had in previous series between the two teams when the West Indies had won fourteen of their previous fifteen matches against England.

TONY COZIER

It was a tense rest day. Was there any way that England could now have their first victory over the West Indies for sixteen years cruelly taken from them at this stage? That evening the worst fears of the team and their supporters were realised as heavy rain swept down on Kingston from the Blue Mountains, turning the streets into rivers. In the morning it was apparent that it had also turned Sabina Park into a quagmire. The covers had leaked on the bowlers' run-ups as well and despite four inspections by the umpires and a wait till four o'clock in the afternoon, there could be no play that day. The usually fierce Jamaican sun which might quickly have dried the ground had failed to put in an appearance at all, so there was many an anxious glance up at the mountains that evening. Hotel curtains twitched early the next morning, too, as the England team and its adherents surveyed the weather. They need not have worried. It was bright and sunny. Now, was there a danger of a late wag from the tail?

DAVID GOWER *There'll be plenty of people in England at the moment delighted at the progress England have made over these three days but certainly the contrast is here for everyone to see. Four years ago England came here having played well against Australia and full of high hopes and certainly didn't justify any of those hopes. This time round England have come here having been thrashed by Australia at home and have turned the tables completely and turned the form book upside down.*
TONY COZIER *And on the way is Small to . . . he's bowled him. Walsh bowled off-stump playing an extravagant drive, a big drive by Walsh, the off-stump is knocked out of the ground. The West Indies have lost their first wicket for the day. It's 237 for nine with Walsh playing a really extravagant drive and missing, bowled by Small for two and the West Indies losing their first wicket for the morning with Small getting his fourth wicket as Walsh goes back bowled for two. West Indies, who are now ahead by 37, are 237 for nine with Patrick Patterson coming in as the last man.*

Patterson now faces Malcolm and plays it up on the on-side, nice looking shot. Malcolm is away down the wicket. There's a run out chance here. The innings is over as Patterson is run out. A ball played on the on-side, Marshall came through from the non-striker's end, Patterson took off extremely late and in fact was run out by half the length of the pitch as Capel moved in from mid-on to lob the return back to Malcolm. The West Indies innings is over at 240 within 19 minutes of the start of the last day of the match and England will need only 41 runs to win this match and to win their first Test against the West Indies in 16 years since they won the final Test of the 1974 series at the Queen's Park Oval in Port-of-Spain. So they haven't taken long. They haven't been delayed long by the West Indies, 240 all out in their second innings. England require 41.

DAVID GOWER *Well, the bulk of the supporters there in the George Headley stand are all Englishmen come across here to view this Test match and they're on their feet. They're applauding Graham Gooch and his men back in to the dressing rooms. The West Indies innings there ended, should we say, in a bit of a shambles.*

Gladstone Small and Devon Malcolm, the two West Indian born fast bowlers, had taken four wickets apiece and were as thrilled as the rest of the team. For Graham Gooch, the captain who had made his team believe in themselves, the only disappointment was that he was not on the field at the moment of victory, having been caught at backward square-leg six runs short of the target.

CHRISTOPHER MARTIN-JENKINS *So England one wicket down, needing one run to win and it is Ian Bishop who's bowled so well in this second innings and indeed pretty well throughout the match, running in to bowl to Wayne Larkins, 28 not out. One run for England to get the first victory against the West Indies for 16 years. Bishop bowls and Larkins hits him firmly to mid-off. He sets off for a run. Patterson mis-fields and England have won the first Test match at Sabina Park. Past the right hand of Patrick Patterson, they bother only to run the one run although there are a couple more for them if they had wanted, and perhaps appropriately, an appropriate gesture of West Indian sportsmanship, it is West Indians who run on to the field as if to celebrate the victory although I think in fact they may be members of the ground staff making sure the square doesn't get damaged with a one day international here on Saturday. But England have made history. Their first win against the West Indies since April 5th 1974 at Port-of-Spain. An extraordinary record of West Indian domination in that time but all the happier therefore for England to have won by nine wickets here today.*

MAURICE FOSTER *They certainly played as a team. We were told about the preparation coming here to the West Indies and I'm sure that many instilled in them the rigours of the tour, it's going to be a very hard tour coming from England to play against the world champions and I think as underdogs they were prepared. They went out there, they batted with a purpose. They bowled with a tremendous purpose, line, length, and there was a lot of planning. You could see it in this England team and they*

Allan Lamb in fine
fettle after his match-
winning innings in
England's historic win
in Jamaica. It was their
first Test victory over
West Indies since 1974

*deserved to win here at Sabina Park. I personally would like to
offer my congratulations to the England team.*

*We could not believe in the West Indies that this
Gooch was the very retiring and almost shy
character that we had seen here on two previous occasions.
He just hadn't looked captaincy material.*

TONY COZIER

*England's reaction after the win was instructive. Of
course, there were celebrations after 16 barren years,
with Allan Lamb in the vanguard as I recall. But they
weren't prolonged or excessive. England, under Micky
Stewart and Graham Gooch, were in West Indies on
business and there were four Tests remaining and a one-
day international in just 36 hours time. The job was
nowhere near complete.*

CHRISTOPHER MARTIN-JENKINS

The next Test match was to be in Georgetown, Guyana, where
England had not played a Test since 1974. They did not play
one this time, either, as rain flooded the ground at Bourda and
the large storm drains which surround the ground flowed back
onto it. It was an unhappy idle time for both teams and
particularly for Viv Richards who suffered a return of the painful
haemorrhoids which had previously plagued him. He had to stand down
for the third Test in Trinidad and Desmond Haynes took on the
captaincy for the first time.

The pitch at the Queen's Park Oval was green and inviting for the
fast bowlers, but it was not the four in the West Indies side who were to
have first use of it, as Gooch won the toss and put the opposition in.
Even he can scarcely have expected to have such success on that first
morning. In the second over, Greenidge was caught at short-leg off a
lifting ball from Malcolm and in the next, Haynes was caught at slip off
Small. It was 5 for two. An early change brought the nagging accuracy
of Angus Fraser into the attack and he had Richardson caught behind for
8 and Best caught at slip for 10. When Dujon padded up to Small to be
lbw it was 29 for five. The West Indies survived being plunged to even
greater depths when Logie was missed behind the wicket. It was to prove
a costly mistake as he and Hooper took West Indies into the afternoon
with a sixth wicket stand of 63, before David Capel had Hooper caught
behind for 32. Malcolm then got back to business, persuading Ezra
Moseley, in his first Test, and Curtly Ambrose to edge catches to Jack
Russell behind the stumps. The West Indies were back in serious trouble
at 103 for eight. They recovered, to an extent, thanks to a ninth wicket

stand of 74 between Gus Logie and Ian Bishop, the two local boys. Malcolm eventually bowled Bishop for 16 and Logie was caught off Fraser from a shot that looked to be about to bring him a well deserved century. He was last out for 98 and the West Indies had been dismissed in the final session of the first day for 199.

On the second day, Graham Gooch and Wayne Larkins had settled for grim accumulation, with no frills. They started that day with their opening partnership already at 43 and took it to 112 before Ambrose had Larkins caught behind for 54. The same fate befell Alec Stewart, but

England openers Graham Gooch and Wayne Larkins discuss the battle plan during the third Test. The captain had a lot to do with the decision to include Larkins on the tour, and the Northamptonshire batsman rewarded the faith put in him with a defiant 54 in the first innings

those were the only two wickets the West Indies did get that day which ended with England 189 for two, just ten runs behind.

England were still not ahead on the third morning when they lost the wicket of Gooch caught behind off Bishop for 84 which, away from his normal character, had taken him 263 balls and only brought him three boundaries. His departure to the new ball precipitated something of a mini-collapse with England only just in the lead. The hostile Moseley, who, after his participation in a tour of South Africa, had had to wait until the age of 32 for this first Test chance, had Smith caught behind and Rob Bailey caught at short-leg first ball. When Lamb ducked into a bouncer from Bishop and was bowled off the grille of his helmet, three wickets had fallen with the score 214, only 15 runs ahead. Capel, first with Russell for the seventh wicket and then with Fraser for the ninth determinedly accumulated partnerships of 29 and 40 to make sure that the hard work of the first two days would not be wasted. Capel made 40 and the eventual lead was 89.

The West Indies started their second innings already 35 minutes past the official close of play time, but there were only three legitimate balls from the hostile Malcolm before the umpires decided that the remaining 8.5 overs could not be bowled in the gathering gloom. Even so, 11 runs had already come. After the rest day Greenidge and Haynes set about restoring the West Indies position in the match and, indeed, the series. By lunch, they were only 13 runs away from catching up with England's lead and they were still together. Half an hour after the interval a leg-side shot for three from Haynes put them in front, but ten minutes after that Fraser made a ball to Greenindge nip back as he pushed forward and he was lbw for 42. It was 96 for one, but the new West Indies captain was pushing on towards his fifty.

TONY COZIER *In comes Malcolm on the way now to Haynes and Haynes gets a short ball and he pulls it. Magnificent shot, through square-leg, forward of square for four. Short ball and Haynes really hammered it, pulling it in front of square for four. A shot which he has attempted more than once since lunch. He's now finally got hold of it and it came from the middle of the bat, went like a shot from a gun into the fence just in front of square-leg down to the mid wicket area under the soman tree there behind the Geddes Grant stand for four runs. Haynes 45 and the West Indies 100 is raised. 100 for the West Indies in the course of the 35th over of the innings. So back with Malcolm now. Has been aggressive today, Devon Malcolm, and has been fast as well but that one was really punished by Haynes. He's on way now to Haynes and Haynes gets a ball which comes. . . he's out caught! He's caught in the gully off the back of the bat. Haynes trying to turn the ball on the on-side, the ball coming from the back of the bat, just a bit of lift on to it and a easy catch for Lamb in the gully, and the West Indies openers, after adding 96 for the first wicket have gone in successive overs with Haynes caught by Lamb off Malcolm for 46 and after hammering Malcolm through*

David Capel is expressionless as Curtly Ambrose celebrates another wicket, and England are all out for 288

mid-wicket Haynes is caught in the gully. Tried to turn the ball on the on-side and the ball lifted a bit more than he expected and it went off the back of the bat down for a comfortable, lobbed catch to gully where Lamb was stationed. 100 for two the West Indies in over number 35. They're now ahead by just 11 runs and they've now lost both openers.

TREVOR BAILEY And it so often happens that, after a big partnership, both batsmen go and it's a classic case here. It was a nasty delivery. It lifted just that little bit. There is this bite in this wicket for the faster bowlers and we've now got two new batsmen in and they'll have to try to re-establish the situation which at the moment is distinctly dodgy.

TONY COZIER Malcolm, having taken that wicket in the course of his 13th over. He's a big, strong man. Gooch has asked him to do quite a bit of work today but he certainly looks capable of it. Worked on his stamina as in fact all the England team have done since before coming to the West Indies. They went up to Lilleshall, the sports centre. Here's Malcolm now in to Best and Best is rapped on the pad. He's out leg-before. Best out leg-before with a ball which kept low on him. He was on the back foot and Best goes leg-before without scoring to the second ball he received. Umpire Barker's finger going up very swiftly as Best trapped on the back foot. The ball in the opinion of the umpire going to hit the wicket and up went the finger quite quickly. Best, leg-before without scoring. The match has taken on a completely different complexion in the past 10 minutes or so, with three wickets going in the space of four runs. Best leg-before wicket to Malcolm and the West Indies are 100 for three. Yes a good piece of bowling there by Malcolm. It was genuinely quick and to add to Best's problem it kept low, and he was late on the stroke. He was well across the stumps, hit him on the pad and, looking through the glasses, it looked fairly plumb. A great blow struck there by Malcolm and, of course, the game now swinging back in to a most interesting and gripping position.

TREVOR BAILEY Well I would have thought it knocked out all three that. It looked very, very plumb and I don't think there's very much doubt about that one. It kept low. It was a good ball and he was late on it.

TONY COZIER Dujon has been short of runs in fact in recent Test matches. He hasn't had a half century in Test cricket, I was working it out the other day, over the last 12 Tests I think it is. The last time he scored a half century was in England at the Oval in 1988 and he's had five Tests against India here last year. He had five in Australia following that and this is the second Test of the series here and he needs some runs, but this is a ground where he's happiest at. He's got two

Test Match Special

173

*centuries here at the Queen's Park Oval, two out of his five in Test cricket.
Comes in now with the score at 100 for three as Malcolm is on the way to
bowl to him. Comes in now to. . . he's rapped him on the pad. He's bowled
him. He's bowled him first ball, off-stump. So the off-stump hit and Dujon
is out first ball playing back. A rather non-descript shot by Dujon. The
ball was through before he could get either the pad or the bat down. Dujon
bowled by Malcolm without scoring. Malcolm is running through the West
Indies' middle order here. He's now got three wickets and the West Indies
are 100 for four with a first-ball dismissal, Dujon bowled by Malcolm
without scoring.*

GERRY GOMEZ *And pandemonium I would say here, for the game has
certainly take on a most dramatic turn. Where a few minutes ago it was 90
odd for no wicket and then 100 for one and then three very important
wickets taken and Malcolm, really with his tail up. What fine bowling.
This one was well directed. It was a shade outside the off-stump, cutting
back and again beat him with sheer pace.*

Three wickets falling in four balls with the score at exactly 100 had
dramatically changed the game, with the West Indies now 11 runs on
but with four wickets down. There was still batting potential there,
though, and Logie and Richardson now put on 42 for the fifth wicket
either side of the tea interval, before Logie, cutting at Malcolm, was
caught at slip. Richardson, too, was caught at slip, off Small. Two more
wickets fell with the score at 200 and Malcolm had taken his first five-
wicket Test haul. He had to wait till the following morning to make it
six, when he had the last man, Courtney Walsh, lbw to end the innings
at 239 in the third over of the final day. Malcolm had taken six for 76.

> We had heard reports that Malcolm was quick on his
> day, but that he had so few of those days, and he
> was wild and all over the place. So he was a surprise
> package.
>
> TONY COZIER

England had 91 overs to score 151 runs, which should not have been too
difficult a task. Gooch and Larkins had put on 27 when Moseley was
introduced to the attack after a wayward start by Ambrose, and Larkins
was caught behind for 7. But the biggest blow to England came in
Moseley's next over.

CHRISTOPHER MARTIN-JENKINS *One fifty-one, England's target. They're 37
for one now. As Moseley comes in again with his even approach past
umpire Cumberbach and bowls to Gooch. That's a nasty bouncer which. . .
Gooch drops his bat as it hit him on the glove and he's hurt. Ball lobbed
up had there been short-leg, Logie, there he might well have caught it.*

Hit him on the back of the hand and this would be a tragedy for England now if their captain were to have broken a finger there. He's certainly hurt and. . .

TREVOR BAILEY *That was a good, good bouncer, a really nasty one.*

CHRISTOPHER MARTIN-JENKINS *He's a very good bowler, Ezra Moseley, isn't he, and I think the way he's bowled in this his first Test match, he would have been a Test player before now had he not chosen, at a time of very considerable fast bowling strength, to seek his fortune for a time in South Africa. Laurie Brown, the England physio has come on. The ball looks to have hit Gooch. . . oh dear I'm afraid that's a broken finger by the look of the way Gooch winced in agony there.*

Gooch is in some pain and I've got a horrible feeling that what England dreaded happening bringing only two opening batsmen, may just have happened. A broken bone and the last person in the entire side of course that it should have happened to is Graham Gooch.

TREVOR BAILEY *Yes he's going off.*

CHRISTOPHER MARTIN-JENKINS *He's going to go off and this is cruel luck.*

The crucial moment of the series. It's the Trinidad Test and a nasty bouncer from Ezra Moseley hits Graham Gooch on the glove, breaking the England captain's hand in the process

Test Match Special

175

Gooch has enough presence of mind to have a word with Alec Stewart before he goes off but I fear the worst there. I fear a broken bone.
TREVOR BAILEY *Yes it was. It got up from only just short of a length. He got right behind the ball in to line. He has bowled some nasty ones, lifters, since he's come on, Moseley, he's looked far more hostile than Ambrose who really didn't bowl at all well, and Haynes must be desperately sorry that he didn't open with Moseley rather than Ambrose.*

As Gooch went off to hospital for an X-ray, more bad luck was in the offing for England. In the last over before lunch, as Lamb and Stewart, at 73 for one seemed to be cruising to a victory well inside the distance, rain started to fall. Cruelly for England, during the interval, it started to get really heavy.

No one had forecast the rain coming that afternoon. No one even saw it coming over and at lunch I am sure the West Indians on the ground felt that it was all over bar the shouting. They had plenty of wickets in hand and the West Indies bowling was not threatening at all.

TONY COZIER

It was four hours before a reluctant ground staff had dragged the covers off and the umpires had pronounced the ground fit for play. The West Indian players did not agree, but they had now a nominal 30 overs to bowl and England had 78 runs to get to go two up in the series. The West Indies fast bowlers, with Moseley the worst, now put on a macabre pantomime of a game of cricket slowing the game down to such an extent that it quickly became apparent that they had no intention of bowling as many as half that number of overs before darkness fell. News came from the England dressing room that Gooch's hand was not broken, just badly bruised. In the aftermath of the match this was to be revealed as having been a ploy to make the West Indies believe that he would be available to bat again.

The pitch had been freshened up and the bowlers, on the rare occasions when they bowled a ball, were proving quite a handful. Walsh had Alec Stewart caught at third man, Robin Smith lbw to a shooter and Rob Bailey bowled playing back. Five overs after the re-start (which had taken three-quarters of an hour) England were 85 for four, but the West Indies seemed unable to see their own chance of a victory. The statutory twenty overs in the last hour did not start until a quarter of an hour after the scheduled close-of-play time. Allan Lamb was out in the second of those overs, lbw to the rapid Ian Bishop for 25. At 106 for five, the target was tantalisingly only 45 runs away and 18 overs remained to be bowled. The new batting pair were David Capel and Jack Russell. At 115, Capel was missed at slip as he cut at Bishop. With 13 overs to go only 32 runs more were needed, but the light was fading fast and it would be pitch dark in minutes. One more run came off the next over. 31 were needed off a theoretical 14 overs.

TONY COZIER *Now the batsmen are consulting. They're looking towards the dressing room. They want instructions, do we continue or do we go off? Is the match worth continuing to try and win it? Shall we come off and go for the draw? There's a long talk. Hussain came out, had a word with the batsmen. He's gone back in with a message. The umpires are waiting now.*
DAVID GOWER *Well there's confusion all round.*
TONY COZIER *Capel is asking, he's looking back to the dressing room. He can't see. Bat on. I'm sure they're going to say. Capel is going towards the dressing room. I don't think he's finished yet. Yes it looks as if they're going off. Yes they have decided to go off. So the match has well shall we say ended. We have had so many twists and turns in this match. Who knows in a while the sun could come out brightly but the umpires in fact are now pulling the stumps. So that is the end of this absolutely enthralling, bizarre almost, Test match. The third Cable and Wireless Test of the series ending in a draw with England 31 runs away from their target of 151 in their second innings. Five wickets down and therefore five wickets standing and the match has ended in a draw. So the players even to the end, the confusion, the twists and the turns which we've had all the way through continued with the batsmen in the middle waiting instructions from their captain, from their dressing room to find out whether they should continue or not with umpires having already offered them the option of going off. In the end they looked at the pavilion and they got the signals to come off to settle for the draw.*

The Trinidad Test represented the cruellest deprivation of any side that I have reported on. A malevolent fate decided that England were to be denied.

Ultimately the game left a nasty taste. Of all the disgraceful examples of time wasting in Test cricket the West Indies performance on the final day was the worst. They were like an Italian football side defending a 1-0 lead. To bowl just 17 overs in two hours was indefensible.

I have to report that the England players were much less incensed than the British press and supporters about the time wasting. Perhaps they were honest enough to admit they may have acted in a similar fashion given a reversal of circumstances. I personally like to think otherwise.

England's decision to come off when offered the light was entirely correct, the light was impossible for batting.
CHRISTOPHER MARTIN-JENKINS

FINAL · SCORES

Sabina Park, Kingston, First Test

WEST INDIES - First Innings

C G Greenidge, run out	32
D L Haynes, c & b Small	36
R B Richardson, c Small b Capel	10
C A Best, c Russell b Capel	4
C L Hooper, c Capel b Fraser	20
L V A Richards, lbw b Malcolm	21
P J L Dujon, not out	19
M D Marshall, b Fraser	0
I R Bishop, c Larkins b Fraser	0
C A Walsh, b Fraser	6
B P Patterson, b Fraser	0
Extras (b9, lb3, nb4)	16
Total	164

Fall of wickets: 1-62, 2-81, 3-92, 4-92, 5-124, 6-144, 7-144, 8-150, 9-164
Bowling: Small 15-6-44-1, Malcolm 16-4-49-1, Fraser 20-8-28-5, Capel 13-4-31-2

ENGLAND - First Innings

G A Gooch, c Dujon b Patterson	18
W Larkins, lbw b Walsh	46
A J Stewart, c Best b Bishop	13
A J Lamb, c Hooper b Walsh	132
R A Smith, c Best b Bishop	57
N Hussain, c Dujon b Bishop	13
D J Capel, c Richardson b Walsh	25
R C Russell, c Patterson b Walsh	26
G C Small, lbw b Marshall	4
A R C Fraser, not out	2
D E Malcolm, lbw b Walsh	0
Extras (b23, lb 12, nb12, w1)	48
Total	364

Fall of wickets: 1-40, 2-60, 3-116, 4-288, 5-315, 6-315, 7-325, 8-339, 9-364
Bowling: Patterson 18-2-74-1, Bishop 27-5-72-3, Marshall 18.2-3-46-1, Walsh 27.2-4-68-5, Hooper 6-0-28-0, Richards 9-1-22-0, Best 4-0-19-0

WEST INDIES - Second Innings

C G Greenidge, c Hussain b Malcolm	36
D L Haynes, b Malcolm	14
R B Richardson, lbw b Fraser	25
C A Best, c Gooch b Small	64
C L Hooper, c Larkins b Small	8
L V A Richards, b Malcolm	37
P J L Dujon, b Malcolm	15
M D Marshall, not out	8
I R Bishop, c Larkins b Small	3
C A Walsh, b Small	2
B P Patterson, run out	2
Extras (b14, lb10, nb1, w1)	26
Total	240

Fall of wickets: 1-26, 2-69, 3-87, 4-112, 5-192, 6-222, 7-222, 8-227, 9-237
Bowling: Small 22-6-58-4, Malcolm 21.3-2-77-4, Fraser 14-5-31-1, Capel 15-1-50-0

ENGLAND - Second Innings

G A Gooch, c Greenidge b Bishop	8
W Larkins, not out	29
A J Stewart, not out	0
Extras (lb1, nb3)	4
Total (1 wkt)	41

Fall of wickets: 1-35
Bowling: Patterson 3-1-11-0, Bishop 7.3-0-17-1, Walsh 6-0-12-0

England won by 9 wickets

Gus Logie sinks low to avoid a bouncer during his innings of 98

FINAL · SCORES

Queen's Park Oval, Port-of-Spain, Third Test

WEST INDIES - First Innings

C G Greenidge, c Stewart b Malcolm		5
D L Haynes, c Lamb b Small		0
R B Richardson, c Russell b Fraser		8
C A Best, c Lamb b Fraser		10
P J L Dujon, lbw b Small		4
A L Logie, c Lamb b Fraser		98
C L Hooper, c Russell b Capel		32
E A Moseley, c Russell b Malcolm		0
C E L Ambrose, c Russell b Malcolm		7
I R Bishop, b Malcolm		16
C A Walsh, not out		8
Extras (lb4, nb7)		11
Total		199

Fall of wickets: 1-5, 2-5, 3-22, 4-27, 5-29, 6-92, 7-93, 8-103, 9-177
Bowling: Small 17-4-41-2, Malcolm 20-2-60-4, Fraser 13.1-2-41-3, Capel 15-2-53-1

ENGLAND - First Innings

G A Gooch, c Dujon b Bishop		84
W Larkins, c Dujon b Ambrose		54
A J Stewart, c Dujon b Ambrose		9
A J Lamb, b Bishop		32
R A Smith, c Dujon b Moseley		5
R J Bailey, c Logie b Moseley		0
D J Capel, c Moseley b Ambrose		40
R C Russell, c Best b Walsh		15
G C Small, lbw b Bishop		0
A R C Fraser, c Hooper b Ambrose		11
D E Malcolm, not out		0
Extras (b10, lb9, nb16, w3)		38
Total		288

Fall of wickets: 1-112, 2-125, 3-195, 4-214, 5-214, 6-214, 7-243, 8-244, 9-284
Bowling: Ambrose 36.2-8-59-4, I Bishop 31-6-69-3, Walsh 22-5-45-1, Hooper 18-5-26-0, Moseley 30-5-70-2

WEST INDIES - Second Innings

C G Greenidge, lbw b Fraser		42
D L Haynes, c Lamb b Malcolm		45
R B Richardson, c Gooch b Small		34
C A Best, lbw b Malcolm		0
P J L Dujon, b Malcolm		0
A L Logie, c Larkins b Malcolm		20
C L Hooper, run out		10
E A Moseley, c Lamb b Malcolm		26
C E L Ambrose, c Russell b Fraser		18
I R Bishop, not out		15
C A Walsh, lbw b Malcolm		1
Extras (b2, lb13, nb12, w1)		28
Total		239

Fall of wickets: 1-96, 2-100, 3-100, 4-100, 5-142, 6-167, 7-200, 8-200, 9-234
Bowling: Small 21-8-56-1, Malcolm 26.2-4-77-6, Fraser 24-4-61-2, Capel 13-3-30-0

ENGLAND - Second Innings

G A Gooch, retired hurt		18
W Larkins, c Dujon b Moseley		7
A J Stewart, c Bishop b Walsh		31
A J Lamb, lbw b Bishop		25
R A Smith, lbw b Walsh		2
R J Bailey, b Walsh		0
D J Capel, not out		17
R C Russell, not out		5
Extras (b2, lb7, nb6)		15
Total (5 wkts)		120

Fall of wickets: 1-27, 2-74, 3-79, 4-85, 5-106,
Bowling: Ambrose 6-0-20-0, I Bishop 10-1-31-1, Walsh 7-0-27-3, Hooper 18-5-26-0, Moseley 10-2-33-1

Match drawn

Index

Names in **bold** type indicate commentators. Page numbers in **bold** indicate interviews; in *italic*, photographs

Photographic Acknowledgements

We are grateful to everyone who supplied photographs for the book. Special thanks go to Annabel Eagar, Eve Horan, Roger Mann and Abigail Sims for their invaluable help.

Aldus Archive 18-19, back cover
Allsport 12
Associated Press 22, 38, 39, 72, 73, 78, 82-83
Simon Bruty/Allsport 159

Patrick Eagar front cover (main photo), 85, 92, 93, 98-99, 100, 104, 106, 112-113, 121, 122, 146, 155, 162
David Frith 48
Hulton Picture Company 10, 16, 23, 25, 28, 29, 32, 34-35, 37, 41, 64, 66-67, 69, 70-71, 76, 79, 87, 88, 97
Roger Mann 15, 21, 27, 30, 33, 43, 44-45, 49, 52-53, 55, 56, 58, 61,

62-63, 65
Bob Martin/Allsport 165
Graham Morris 139, 142-143, 154, 156-157, 175
Adrian Murrell/Allsport front cover (inset photos), 101, 107, 108, 115, 118, 119, 125, 128, 130, 132, 133, 136, 137, 140, 144, 145, 160, 161, 163, 170, 171, 172-173, 178-179
S&G Press Agency 51